CONVERSATIONS WITH A WIDOW

CONVERSATIONS WITH A WIDOW

Speaking the Unspoken

GAIL BAYRON

Indy Pub

*To those of us who've had our worlds turned upside down
who find ourselves vulnerable to life's storms, to its lies, its
pain, its coldness*

And to its surprises, its healing, its beauty, its warmth.

Contents

TWO
FAITH

THREE
FRIENDS

FOUR
TRADITIONS

FIVE
OTHER SECONDARY LOSSES

Acknowledgements

To my millennial daughter, Kristyn, quietly going about the business of writing and publishing her own stories. Thank you for sharing with me your experiences – good and bad – in your own book writing and publishing journey. I'm grateful to be the beneficiary of lessons you've learned, as well as to all the tech stuff you've picked up along the way. Thank you for your patience with me as you held space for the gap between you telling me something and me telling you the same thing later when my own experience afforded me the context on which to hang your earlier words. I may not get there quickly, but I eventually do. ("That's what she said." Yeah, I knew you'd say that.)

To Cari Cook who provided me with a demonstrable answer to the question, "Does anybody barter for services anymore?" You were the first one to lay eyes on all the different parts of my manuscript, to my raw and honest grief. Your edits helped me fill in some blanks and add details and/or depth to my stories, and called me out when I was the only one who knew what I was talking about. I'm grateful for your non-judgemental read of my story, and for the grace I felt from you as we worked on this project together.

To Amber Lea Taylor-Thomas, thank you for investing time and energy in editing for a brand new author. Your responses to my stories have made me feel seen. And now I know how to make a proper em dash.

To Kathy Platt who has been a beacon of light allowing me to see my true self as it has slowly revealed itself, and has borne witness as these truths took root in my being and manifested in my life. Your insights and gentle guidance in every step of this widow's journey – even the hard steps that I didn't want to take – have been integral to the whole process.

To Joann Filomena whose coaching gave me tools to help me move from a place of just surviving to one of thriving. You showed how my thoughts, emotions, and actions are all connected. You taught me to think about what I think about, and gave me permission to think different thoughts so I could feel different emotions and live a different life.

Introduction

Widowhood. Welcome to the conversation.

What's that? You haven't heard about this conversation? Yeah, I hadn't either – until I became a widow. Even then it was hard to find.

Nobody wants to talk about it. It's an unpleasant conversation that we have learned to make brief, to side-step, or to avoid altogether.

So where did that leave me as a new widow? With lots of questions and no real answers, that's where. I didn't know many other widows, and the ones I did know were either older or they just seemed to have everything together. I couldn't tell that there was anything different about them after their loss, so I never thought to have a conversation with them about it.

I had these little experiences... I thought I was the only one experiencing them. Like losing all of my voicemails from Rod (my husband) ... that shouldn't be such a big deal, should it? And the start of the new season of the show we used to watch together ... that shouldn't make me cry, right? And does anyone else ever have a full-on meltdown, complete with a crying-screaming match, while installing a new cable box? Anyone?

I'd heard about the five stages of grief as explained by Elisabeth Kübler-Ross* (denial, anger, bargaining, depression, acceptance). They seemed pretty straightforward and clear-cut; I should be able to tell once I've completed one stage and entered the next. I could just bide my time until I got to that final stage of acceptance – which I equated to getting back to 'normal' – and all would be well once again. Except I couldn't tell which stage I was in.

As I understood and applied these stages to my own situation, I figured out that while I might be entering the anger stage in processing my primary loss (Rod's death), I might just be gaining awareness of a secondary loss (like losing all his voicemails). Because the impact of this secondary loss is new, I'd be in the first stage – denial – for this particular loss, alongside the second stage – anger – of losing Rod. As the primary loss continued to process and move through the stages, new secondary losses would continue to emerge, each starting at the first stage. No wonder I couldn't tell which stage I was in – I was in all of them at the same time, starting the process anew with each secondary loss as it revealed itself! That's enough to make anyone feel like they're going crazy!

I did some research to find out more about these stages, and I learned that these stages weren't as clear-cut as I thought they were. I learned that the author, Elisabeth Kübler-Ross, meant that these stages describe what a person goes through when they find out they have a terminal illness. It was never meant to be applied generally to grief.

Nevertheless, the framework of the five stages of grief had afforded me some semblance of order to the chaos of grief that I felt. Realizing that that framework – with its specific and seemingly achievable end of acceptance – was never meant to apply to me, I added feeling lost and alone to crazy.

Mine has been a journey of questions. Some answers I figured out on my own. Others I found with the help of resources (some of which are included in the Resources section at the end of this book) that were able to either provide an answer or put me in touch with someone who could. And that someone was always another widow.

I hope I can be that someone for you, not only sharing my experience, but also being present with you as you walk your own path.

Many of the things I began to question after Rod died are related to me being raised in the USA in the 1960s and 70s. I had certain expectations about relationships and my place in the world; male/female expectations and roles were pretty well defined in my growing up. So learning to be a woman alone – without a man – at age 51 seemed an impossible undertaking, one that I had little direction and less interest in pursuing, though I understood its necessity.

Many of my long held religious beliefs also came into question with Rod's cancer, and his death. I'll be talking about some of the spiritual insights, epiphanies, and revelations I've made along the way. If something resonates with you, follow it; if it conflicts with your beliefs, that's okay. Your stories and experiences will undoubtedly be different from mine.

These are not presented as universal truths, they are simply my story – nothing more.

Death is no respecter of persons; you might have been with your partner for a short time or spent over half a century together. Maybe you grew up in an environment that encouraged independence and autonomy, or maybe you were protected and/or shielded from the world. Regardless of these different life circumstances, it is my hope that you will find a common thread in our experiences as widows.

This is not intended to be a "How-To" manual, nor is it my intention to tell you that my solution is the best solution, or even that it is the only one. It is my intention and desire to open up a conversation about secondary losses and to give you insight into how one widow dealt with these losses.

To that end, I've arranged this book by grouping my experiences as they relate to the topics of Identity, Friends, Faith, Holidays and Other Special Days, and Other Secondary Losses. To help give context for what changed in my life and the significance of those changes, I've included stories about what my life was like before I met Rod, what our life together was like, and what my life has been like since he died.

You can read straight through this book like a memoir, though it is not a chronological account of my experiences. You can also browse through the topics and use this book as a reference as you find yourself asking similar questions.

As I share my experiences with you, know that I hold space for you on your own journey. I hope you can feel my presence, right there beside you, whenever you are ready to take your next step – or your first.

And most of all I hope that you will come away from this book with the knowledge that you are not alone. And you are not crazy.

Be gracious with yourself.

And remember to breathe.

*Find out more information about Elisabeth Kubler-Ross and the Five Stages of Grief at https://www.ekrfoundation.org/

ONE

Identity

There's this moment when you're sure you're
about to die. And then, you're born.

It's terrifying.

Right now, I'm a stranger to myself.

There's echoes of who I was, and this sort
of call towards who I am. And I have to
hold my nerve and trust all these new
instincts, shape myself towards them.

I'll be fine. In the end. Hopefully."

Doctor Who (TV series), "The Woman Who
Fell To Earth" 2018

Before Rod

As a little girl, I could imagine what my grown-up life would look like. Growing up in the 1960s and 70s, my role in life was laid out for me. Expectations of a woman were clearly demonstrated to me. Sure, there was room for some variation, but the cultural norm dictated that I would graduate high school, go to college (mostly to find a husband), get married, have kids, and live happily ever after.

Becoming a wife was the prescribed way to achieve my

happily ever after and to fulfill these expectations. Therefore, my goal was to find a husband.

I observed this role being fulfilled in many of the TV shows I watched as a little girl; women like Carol Brady, Maureen Robinson, and Samantha Stevens (The Brady Bunch, Lost in Space, and Bewitched, respectively) all assumed their place under the authority and leadership of their husbands. These influences and examples in the media of what my role should be were very ... influential.

There were a few shows on the periphery that did not reflect the "proper" female role, but those were not prominent in my world. They were shows about successful, independent, single women like Shirley Partridge, Ann Marie and Mary Richards (The Partridge Family, That Girl, and The Mary Tyler Moore Show respectively), but somehow those didn't resonate with me. Perhaps it was because all of my real life examples looked more like the former than the latter, and that ideal outweighed any other notion of what life might look like.

I internalized these socially established roles so completely that I believed they were my own desires. I didn't desire a career or money. I desired a family and a relationship with a husband. There were no other options that appealed to me in any way. There really was no other pursuit for me; this path was ingrained in me and I eagerly accepted it. I *wanted* to be a wife. I *wanted* to be a mother. As a little girl, when someone asked me what I wanted to be when I grew up, these were my answers, whether or not I stated them quite that succinctly.

So I happily accepted this role that was modeled for me in my home, my friends' homes, and in the media I consumed.

It was reinforced in conversations, in lyrics, and in plot lines. I bought into the script. I believed it suited me well, and I looked forward to one day becoming Wife.

At the core of my being, I believed that to be a woman was to be a wife. They were synonymous in my world; there was no distinction between Woman and Wife.

And I understood that Wife needed Husband in order to fulfill her role. Without Husband, there is no Wife; Husband gives context to Wife. I needed a husband so that I could be a wife and thereby fulfill my role as a woman.

As a grown-up, Wife would be how I would interface with the world and everyone in it. It was how I would know who I was; it would define my responsibilities in the home, my place in the world, and my purpose in life. That role would become my identity, merged into a single entity that eventually became Rod's Wife.

2

Rod's Wife

My grown-up life turned out pretty much the way I'd imagined it. Given the influences and environment that I grew up in and that I adopted that narrative as my own, I was very happy when I got to step into the role of Wife. After all, it was what I believed I was created to do, who I believed I was designed to be.

And I didn't have to wait very long to do it!

My mom died when I was 12 years old, and my dad remarried when I was 16, near the end of my sophomore year of high school. We moved to a different city to be closer to her work, and that put me in a different school in a different district.

On the first day of school, I arrived on my new campus an hour early to walk my class route, which only took a few minutes. So I sat on a courtyard bench near my first class until I saw the teacher unlock and go into the classroom. When I entered the classroom a few minutes later, there was only one other student there; I took a seat in the middle row on the other side of the room. I watched as other students came in.

About the fourth or fifth to file in was a cute boy. He was kinda skinny and not very tall, had tan skin and kissable-looking lips. He had acne, and his hair was kinda long and tall at the same time and looked like it needed a wash.

He scanned the room, probably looking for someone he might know. Our eyes met briefly; I was in love! He sat down just one seat over from me, making my heart race. (He told me much later that he chose that seat because it was where he sat for a different class he had in that classroom last semester.)

A few minutes later, a girl came in and sat in front of me. She and the cute boy greeted each other – she knew him! I needed to make friends with her so I could ask her about this cute boy. But my attempts to glean relevant information were thinly veiled. She told me his name was Rod, then promptly advised me against pursuing a relationship with him, saying it would never work between us. (Despite my completely ignoring her advice, Naomi and I became good friends.)

By the holidays Rod and I were flirting with each other, and getting to know one other. Turns out he already had two girlfriends on campus and three girlfriends in three other cities. (How he managed that without a car is still a mystery to me.) This is probably the reason for Naomi's advice.

On March 2 of our Junior year, he asked me to go steady (yes, steady – it was 1979!) and gave me his class ring to wear on a chain around my neck. By that time, he had broken up with all his other girlfriends and chosen to be exclusively with me. Two months later, he randomly said, "I'm gonna marry you." I just laughed it off, but I think I knew in my heart he was serious. Maybe that was because I wanted him to be.

At the end of our senior year, Rod's family was going to a restaurant to celebrate his graduation. He invited me to join them, but he had an ulterior motive – he was going to officially propose. I eagerly accepted and could not stop smiling and showing off my engagement ring.

Dating in the late '70s and early '80s was interesting. Most of our dates involved dinner and a movie, and most of the movies being released at the time were slasher movies – the original Halloween, the first Friday the 13th, etc. I'm not a fan of the horror flick to begin with, but I was definitely a fan of Rod. If that's where he wanted to take me for our dates, then that's where I was going. Little did I know that watching all those movies would scar me; going into a movie theater – for any movie – would send me into a panic for a couple of decades!

I was a June bride. We got married under a gazebo in a garden two years after our engagement (almost to the day). We had our first baby almost two years later ... and the rest of the steps fell right into place. My life was going exactly according to plan. I was taking all the right steps in the right order – for the most part.

I knew my new role. I knew what was expected of me, and I happily did it. It was the only life I ever wanted, the only life I was prepared for, and the only life I thought I'd ever live.

Think of a bird that hatches in a nest and learns to fly. He only ever lives in the air. Or a fish that emerges from an egg in the water – he lives his whole life in the water. Neither the bird nor the fish is interested in what the other's life is like or what it might be like to live in a different environment. Each has very little, if any, knowledge about the other – and even less curiosity. A bird is a bird for its whole life. It will always be a bird and it will always live in the air. Likewise, a fish is a fish for its whole life. It will always be a fish and it will always live in the water.

In a similar way, I was happy in my environment, in my life and in my role; I was neither curious about nor interested in looking at – or for – anything different. This life was the water I swam in.

As far as I was concerned, there was one definition of wife – one way to be a woman – and I was living it! Even if I wasn't consciously aware of it, I measured every other woman by my definition. If I saw a woman who didn't live out my definition, I didn't think she was a "proper" woman. I never considered that she just found a different way to be a woman – that was simply not my thought in my head.

I liked Rod's Wife, and I liked being her. She was who Rod loved and who he built his life with. Rod's Wife was protected and provided for by him. She was safe, and she knew she would be loved forever.

3

Identity Shock

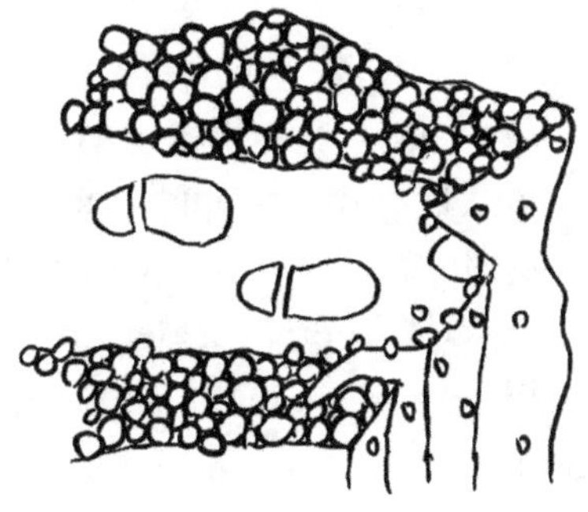

Merriam-Webster defines culture shock in this way: "a sense of confusion and uncertainty sometimes with feelings of anxiety that may affect people exposed to an alien culture or environment without adequate preparation" (https://www.merriam-webster.com/dictionary/culture%20shock). It is when you find yourself in a place where the cultural/social norms are different from your own. Because you are unfamiliar with the local culture, you continue to operate out of your own worldview, expectations and norms. You can see that things are different, but, as Merriam-

Webster puts it, you lack "adequate preparation" to deal with or respond to what you are seeing and experiencing.

I experienced culture shock when I moved from California to Texas when our oldest was just 14 months old. One of the things I was not prepared for was the difference in climate – adapting to the weather is a thing! I had to learn the necessities of living in a desert climate, you know, like always having a bottle of water with you – staying hydrated is really important here! I never had to worry about that in California. I had to not only learn a different way of existing in my new environment, but also with the people in it. Texas has its own social norms; I had to learn a new way of interacting with people, and how to use Southern vernacular.

In a similar way, I went through identity shock when Rod died. Is that a thing – identity shock? Because if it is, that's what I experienced. There was definitely confusion and uncertainty. I could no longer move through the world in a way that was comfortable and familiar to me. That way of living and existing in the world was becoming alien to me. I could see that my new landscape necessitated new habits, a different way to move through it. But I was unprepared, in any useful way, to know what those new habits might be, or what those ways might look like.

The identity that was in crisis was my role as Wife *because* that role *was* my identity. The result of losing that role was that I lost my sense of self. I didn't know how to be anyone other than Wife. I never needed to. I was never interested in knowing.

I was finding that things that had had purpose and meaning no longer did. The things that I just knew and took for granted that directed my days without announcement or conscious thought suddenly didn't exist.

Without that role telling me what time to have dinner ready, how would I know when to start cooking? In fact, dinner time suddenly seemed arbitrary. *Well if I'm not eating dinner at six o'clock then what time am I eating dinner? Or am I eating dinner at all, because that's an option now.* It's like all of a sudden 'dinner time' became meaningless. I didn't know what kind of person doesn't eat dinner at 6 pm.

Without that role to direct me, I didn't know what to do with myself. It's like walking through a crosswalk when there's cars stopped there – with people watching you, you forget how to walk! Then you have to think about how to walk – *Do my hips swing? How do my arms move? Are my steps the right length – what is the right length for a step? Am I walking too slow – or too fast?*

Yeah, identity shock describes it pretty well. My identity was so intertwined with my role as wife – which was determined by my gender – and all of it was just gone. Moving through life in the way I always had no longer made sense, but I didn't know how else to move. I had no context for what I was supposed to do or how to exist in this new world. I didn't even know where to begin. So I continued to move through my world in the only way I knew how, continuing to do all the things Wife did.

But I was not Wife. Does not-Wife really need to fix up her hair or be concerned about how she looks? Does she still need to be cute and feminine if she's not interested in attracting the attention of anybody? These are, after all, things that I did for Rod as Wife.

So that part of my identity was gone, along with my identity as a whole. Wife was who I was. And it was quite a shock to find myself in "an alien environment."

When I first got to Texas, I just kind of existed here. Eventually I learned to adapt to my new environment and to the input I was getting. While it didn't feel like it at the time, looking back I can say that this was a mild version of culture shock. Language wasn't a barrier, just fodder for awkwardness. And while it took a hot minute (pun intended), I got used to carrying a water bottle and even picked up a Texas twang.

I did that with my identity, too, you know? I'd been kind of just existing – compensating, becoming familiar with Widowland. As I gained new insights, learned new habits, and adapted to a new vernacular, my identity began to shift.

But I hated this new identity that was emerging if for no other reason that she wasn't Rod's Wife. Rod and I had a good life together and a promising future ahead of us. The more my identity shifted, the farther away I felt from Rod and the only life I'd ever really known. Or wanted.

I knew the shift was necessary because my role as wife had been fulfilled. Rod's Wife died with Rod, and she no longer existed. I can't still be Wife without Husband. My efforts to continue as I always had proved to be futile.

So here I was in my early 50s and newly single, wondering what else life might look like, what else Woman might mean.

4

No Longer Rod's Wife

The moment Rod died, Rod's Wife died, too, but I couldn't comprehend all that that meant. I had spent my whole adult life in a role that was basically assigned to me, a role that was dependent upon someone else (husband) to fulfill. I was a subordinate in a hierarchy of men and women, and my duties and functions in that role as wife, even as woman, were predefined.

I thought I would be a wife my whole life. And for some time after his death, I still felt like I was a married woman.

But in practical terms, that role had been completed. I no longer have a husband to be a wife to.

A few months after Rod died, a long time friend of ours told me that I'd have to figure out who Gail is apart from Rod. At the time, I just wanted to slap her face right off her head. How dare she imply that I be anything other than Rod's Wife?!

Deep down I knew this friend was right, but I wasn't ready to face the loss of Rod's Wife – I didn't know who I was apart from Rod's Wife. I had no previous identity or life experience to give me that context. So, for a time after he died, I continued to live like Rod's wife would live, that I would always and forever be Rod's wife. I couldn't accept that that would ever change.

Rod's Wife had been my identity 24/7 since I was 20 years old; I was never not Rod's wife in my adult life. Rod's Wife wasn't *part* of my identity; *it was who I was.* I couldn't imagine (much less handle) thinking about not being Rod's Wife. According to my understanding of cultural expectations at that time, a woman who was not Wife had no purpose, nothing of value to offer to anyone. **If I wasn't Rod's Wife, I – as a person, as a woman – would be superfluous.** It was too overwhelming, too much loss to process all at once.

So I continued as best as I could to live as Rod's Wife. I would follow through with plans Rod and I had already set in place together. I had to. *As long as I held on to being Rod's Wife, I would matter.*

The first plan that I followed through on was going on our trip to Israel.

Rod and I worked in different departments of a non-profit

missions organization, e3 Partners Ministry. In January of 2013, Rod won an expenses-paid trip to Israel in a drawing at our organization's bi-annual international conference. Of the four trips scheduled for that year, we selected one toward the end of summer so we would have ample time to raise funds to cover costs for me to go with him.

It was set, and Rod was so excited. I'm not as fond of traveling as Rod was (mostly because of the flying part), but I was looking forward to sharing this experience with him. He had some specific things he wanted to see and questions he wanted to explore.

His cancer diagnosis came in April. I don't remember how much we had raised by that point, but I do remember that a trip to anywhere was no longer on my radar. We would have to wait to see how this would play out.

By mid-summer, things had not improved, but they hadn't worsened either, which is unusual with pancreatic cancer. We began to talk tentatively about going to Israel, and we decided we'd shoot for the last trip of the year, which was leaving Dec 2.

As we moved into fall, Rod talked to his oncologist about the feasibility of traveling, and he cleared Rod to go. It was a medical mission trip so there would be doctors and nurses traveling with us. In addition, Rod's doctor said that medical facilities in Israel were equal to – if not better than – facilities here in the US, so if there was an emergency of any sort, he had confidence that they'd be able to handle it there. With his doctor's clearance, we made our plans for the December trip.

Rod died on November 22. But Rod's Wife kept to the plan and went to Israel.

We also had plans for our retirement. Rod was going to have a voice-over business, and I was going to interpret for the Deaf. Obviously, Rod's Voice would never come to fruition, but I could still carry on with my part of our plan, so I did. I signed up for the Interpreter for the Deaf program at my local community college, with plans to become a certified ASL interpreter. I began full time classes just nine months after his death.

There were other, smaller plans I was able to carry out as Rod's Wife, but eventually all the plans we made together were either realized or had become no longer relevant or viable. At that point, there was no plan, nothing on the books to give me direction, or even for me to look forward to.

Once again, I was lost.

Somewhere in the third year, there was a turning point when I was able to accept that I was no longer Rod's Wife, that it was necessary for me to change that mindset. By that time, I was no longer operating in all the same ways that I did when he was here. For example, I stopped eating foods that I don't prefer and watching shows that didn't really interest me. He was my reason for doing those things, and more. Without him, there was no point for me to continue in such things.

With that acceptance came a period of this void, this question of if I'm not Rod's Wife, then who am I? I've never really had to answer this question before. I moved from my parents' house to my husband's house, so I never had the need (or opportunity) to discover who I was between being Bob's Daughter and Rod's Wife. My whole life I had been someone else's someone.

I picked up a form of meditation (visualization) after Rod

died as a way to reconnect with my Bible (more about that in Chapter 12). I became curious about the benefits of meditation in general, and I expanded my knowledge and practice of meditation beyond the visualization I used in reading my Bible.

In a particular meditation, I discovered there's this space between the shedding of one identity and the forming of a new one. A vulnerable, sticky, messy space where nothing makes sense but anything is possible.

I envisioned what appeared to be God's hand reaching down and picking me up by my scruff. As I observed myself in the sure grip of God's index finger and thumb, I realized that I was looking at an empty skin, like when you pull off the outer layer of a roasted marshmallow. The 'real' me was the gooey, sticky, inside of the marshmallow that was left behind – undefined, amorphous, vulnerable. There were no defining characteristics, no identifying markers. All I knew at that point was that Rod's Wife was no longer who I was.

This meditation was a month shy of the three year anniversary of Rod's death. It took me that long to be ready to accept the reality that I was no longer Rod's Wife.

That felt like losing Rod all over again.

Rod's Wife didn't like seeing this image of herself as an empty shell. Even though I had known for some time that she could not exist without Rod, I wasn't able to accept this reality. **If I were to allow a new identity to arise, that would necessarily mean the end of Rod's Wife.** It would mean that another link to Rod – one more evidence that he existed in this world – would be gone.

This is the nature of secondary losses. Every time I realize a different aspect of the primary loss or reach an end to something that Rod and I shared, there's one less thing in the world that Rod had a part in, that reflects the life I knew with him. It's a new loss because it's the first time I'm experiencing this aspect of the greater loss. Yes, it was lost the moment he died, but the impact, the reality, of it hadn't been realized until this moment.

It's quite a process, this business of shedding an identity. It's hard work that involves lots of self-reflection, asking my-self Why, and lots of self-discovery. New realizations were not always readily accepted, and dealing with them was some-times shelved until I had the capacity to bear it. And this one – releasing Rod's Wife from my being – had been shelved for three years.

5

No Longer Woman

Because I merged my identity as a woman with my role as wife, it has been extremely difficult for me to separate the two. The fact that I no longer held the role of wife coupled with the fact that I suddenly found myself doing things that I had previously considered a male or husband's role left me in quite a state.

If my gender was my role – and I believed it was – and I was now fulfilling both male and female roles, then I was in the midst of a perfect storm where gender and role collided.

Femaleness was in contrast to maleness. I knew what female was because I knew what male was, just like we know what light is because we know what darkness is.

Since my identity was tied up in my role (or what I do), then in finding myself fulfilling the duties and responsibilities of both roles, I lost the uniqueness of femininity. I lost what it meant to be a woman.

I felt like a genderless automaton as I moved through my world doing what needed to be done. It no longer mattered who used to do it, or who was supposed to do it.

I remember looking in the mirror one day seeing the shape of a woman, but in my mind I had morphed into some neutral being, some person that was neither female nor male.

I didn't feel feminine anymore because I was doing masculine things. But I didn't have the physical strength of a man to do some of the traditionally masculine things by myself.

This is the oddest thing to try to describe. The thing in my life (maleness) that defined my femaleness – which was my identity – was now gone. Like when you turn on the lights, the darkness is gone. Without the masculine in my life, the feminine didn't exist.

The mechanism that differentiated male from female roles was no longer in place in my life. Even though I was still doing traditionally female things, without the contrast of a man I didn't feel like a woman. And even though I was doing male things, fulfilling the male role, I didn't feel like a man either. My body was my only indicator of my gender; without the role of wife, what my body was didn't seem to matter.

As a result, I had lost the reason to pursue feminine things, like smelling good or being soft. Or having the shape of a woman, or dressing in a way that would be attractive. I did those things because of and for Rod. Even though we were married for over 30 years, I still wanted to turn his head by doing those things that brought out my femininity. And my femininity brought out his masculinity. Looking feminine was part of being and feeling like a woman.

But without Rod, I had no reason to smell or look feminine. Not only were the reasons for me to be feminine gone, but I was taking on some traditionally masculine roles out of necessity. I mean, stuff needed to get done, and I was the only one doing it.

I actually had reasons not to be feminine. Earrings and cute shoes don't work well when mowing the yard.

In *Star Trek: The Next Generation*, there was an episode called "The Offspring" (Season 3 Episode 16) where the character Data created an android that was like him – he procreated. When he created this android, it was completely gender neutral. It only had those things that made it an android – arms, legs, a torso, a head, and programming. It didn't have any specific features, other than eyes as a way to see, a mouth to be able to speak, and ears to take in sounds. It was all very utilitarian. There was nothing to distinguish this android as either male or female. When Data presented his progeny with information about maleness and femaleness along with the option to choose one or the other, this entity chose female and was given the name Lal.

I kind of felt like Lal when she was in that neutral state. It wasn't that I didn't have a gender; it's that I had taken on roles of both genders, blurring the gender line in my own mind. There was nothing in my activity to indicate or decide which gender I was because I was fulfilling both gender roles. And to me, role and gender were synonymous, inseparable.

I began to ask myself, *What is Woman without Man? What does it mean to be female without male?*

Without day, rich, or cold, how would you know if it was night, if someone was poor, or if something was hot? How would you know which you were experiencing if the other wasn't there to give contrast?

Perhaps part of my loss of identity as a woman – while it was heavily influenced by my role and what I did – is also connected to intimacy. When Rod put his arms around me, I felt sexy; we just fell into each other like puzzle pieces. I don't know how else to describe it. The way our bodies felt up against each other was just the perfect complement. I wasn't conscious of it at the time; all I knew at the time was that's where I belonged. I fit, it felt right; I was safe and protected.

It wasn't until after he died and I lost my sense of femininity that I appreciated that aspect of it, and I realized that it was his masculinity that brought out and highlighted my femininity.

My daughter Kristyn's first job experience was in an office, and it was quite unique as office jobs go. It was in a small family-owned company. She experienced and observed things about the owner of the company, and because that was her first experience in that environment, she concluded that this is what the owners of companies are like. The small business was co-owned by a husband and wife, and the wife treated each employee as an individual, and she knew each of her staff outside of the office.

Once Kristyn's direct manager completed training her, she trusted her to do what she taught her to do. There was no micromanaging, no double-checking, no following her around keeping tabs. As long as the job got done properly and timely, she really let Kristyn just kind of figure out her own best system to do her job. And if Kristyn asked for a piece of equipment or a larger work table or whatever, her manager made sure she got it. Her concern was less on *how* the job got done but *that* it got done.

Anyway, this first job was a really good experience for Kristyn, and that experience set a precedent in her mind that's what it's like to work in an office. With that as her context, when people would say they worked in an office, she believed they had it pretty good. She just assumed that their workplace and their relationships with their superiors were like hers had been. Because that was her only experience; it was her only context.

It wasn't until years after leaving that job that she began to realize that not all office environments are as good as hers had been. It took hearing stories from others about their experiences working in an office for her to really appreciate the uniqueness and the specialness of the environment of her first job.

So in that same sense my experience as Rod's Wife set a precedent for me: *This is what marriage looks like. This is what intimacy is like. This is what it looks like to be a wife, what it feels like to be a woman.*

Of course, I understood cognitively that not all marriages were like mine, but mine was the bar by which I measured them all. My experience would set the context for what I thought about these things. It wasn't until after Rod died that I began to grasp the reality – beyond my mental assent – that a marriage could be defined and lived differently than how I experienced it.

This is a really hard one to describe.

Ok, here's an illustration: If you always wear shoes, you won't know what it's like to walk barefoot – to feel the softness of a carpet or the prickliness of walking on a pebble road or the squishiness of walking on wet grass. As a result of always wearing shoes, the bottoms of your feet are soft and tender.

When you first take off shoes and start walking barefoot, boy, those tootsies feel everything! Every little thing on the ground will poke, scrape, and jab at the tender soles.

You suddenly become aware of – and miss – all the things you didn't appreciate about your shoes. You didn't realize how well your shoes had been keeping your feet protected all this time. You didn't realize how dirty your feet could get without shoes, or what it felt like to step on something sharp or hard or hot. Because you never experienced life without shoes.

Maybe what you looked for in your shoes had been limited to appearance and fit. You wanted your shoes to be comfortable and look good, but that may have been all you focused on because that's what was important to you. You didn't need to worry about all the things you were stepping on that your shoes were protecting your feet from – they just did it. You didn't need to consider if that concrete would be hot, or whether the ground would be muddy or squishy. You didn't have to worry about the safety of your feet because you had shoes.

You know cognitively that concrete gets hot, and you could see that pebbles were pokey. You could see that the grass was muddy or the dirt was squishy. You could feel that snow is cold if you touch it with your hands. I mean, you know these things to be true, but your feet have never experienced them directly.

So the first time you take your shoes off and you walk on hot concrete, that's gonna be a pretty big shocker. Your feet are not prepared to protect themselves from the hazards of all the different surfaces you walk on.

When Rod died, I was like those tender feet. There were things about life, and my identity and role, that I just never had to think about. I was aware that other ways of living existed, but I never had to think about them because they were not part of my experience. I was protected. Rod shielded me from certain things, and I never had to consider what any of them would be like because they just weren't part of my world.

Wife was the shoes my Woman was wearing; when those "shoes" came off, I was exposed, and I felt everything. I was pretty raw when that role was first stripped from me. I was unprepared to go barefoot.

Everything about my identity as a woman was tied to my role as wife. It wasn't just my identity as a woman, but as a human being. I really had no idea who I was apart from Rod. We met when we were 16 – I hadn't even finished growing up yet. I hadn't had a chance to figure myself out as just myself.

I lost what it meant to be a woman because my role was so intertwined with it. My role was determined by my gender as a woman, and my role was my identity.

I'm now aware that who I am is much broader than my body and my physical attributes. Who I am extends beyond the fact that I am a female, and there are things about me that don't have anything to do with my gender.

Having released the role of wife, I was able to see myself as a human being who happens to be in a female body. I want to look cute and smell good because I want to (not because it's what I'm supposed to do), and I have learned that I actually do want to be soft to my own touch. Not to be attractive to (or to attract) anyone, but simply because those things make me happy.

I'm coming to the understanding that Woman is a part of who I am; it's a single aspect of my complete identity. It is just the body I happen to be in as I move through and interact with the world. It's the container where 'who I am' lives.

I can now focus on the 'who I am' part.

6

Forming A New Identity

How does one go about forming a new identity? This was quite the conundrum for me. The identity I had lived was one that was curated for me; I chose it because it was the only acceptable option presented to me, and I proceeded to conform myself to its directives.

This process of forging a new identity feels more like I'm uncovering who was underneath, rediscovering who I was before Rod's Wife, and allowing those discoveries to show me who I truly am rather than deciding who I want to be and fitting myself into another mold.

I am learning that identity is wrapped up in values rather than gender or role. I will move through life and interact with the world according to my personal values, whether I realize it or not. I may say I have a set of values, but if they are not intrinsic to my identity, I will not move according to those stated values organically. How I move through the world when I'm not thinking about it, that's where my true values are revealed, and I believe that's where identity is.

So discovering who I am is really a question of discovering what my personal values are – those intangibles that are most important to me. Those are the things that will influence what (and how) I think about things and the decisions I make – how I move through and interact with the world. These values are the foundation of my worldview.

Whether I view the world as a scary, hard place where I have to scrape for everything, or a bright place full of opportunity and abundance, I'm going to move through it in a way that reflects that belief. How I view the world is going to determine what I think and say, who I trust, and how tightly I hold to things.

So my worldview and the values that I hold are reflected in how I exist in the world. These are what define who I am.

I'm a fan of the British show, Doctor Who. After the Doctor regenerated (Season 2, Episode 0), the tenth Doctor didn't know what this newly regenerated version of himself would be like. As he moved through the episode in his newly regenerated self, he paid attention to what he said and did to help himself figure out what his new iteration was going to be like. He became an observer of himself.

Like the Doctor, I've learned to become an observer of myself. Instead of trying to recapture who I had been, recontextualizing what is, or even by trying to fit myself into a different curated identity, I started to pay attention to my own thoughts and actions. And I began to ask myself why I did, said, or responded in the way that I did. The answers to these questions helped me to discover how I view the world and what's important to me.

I've noticed that kindness, and how it connects us as human beings, is important to me. When people are mean to each other and have no regard for the hurt they cause to others, it makes me sad.

The pandemic in 2020 revealed to me just how connected human beings are. I mean, how can a single virus infect the entire planet in three months' time? There had been enough connections made between people just going about their business in that short span of time to completely infect the entire globe.

We are also connected in ways that are not so obvious; it's not only *what* we do, but *how* we do it. We do have an impact on others, even if it's not quite as obvious as the spreading of a virus.

I've been out shopping and walked by somebody who just has a grumpy, mad face, and is grumbling under their breath. Have you ever seen this person? I mean, I knew they were having a bad day, or at least a bad moment, and when I saw that, it affected me. In that moment I might be like, *Oh! I'm gonna avoid that person!* and I may decide to go down a different aisle. I might mirror their bad mood, making me a little less pleasant when I get home.

But I've also seen people singing in the aisle as they're shopping, exuding joy. I might be like, *Wow! That person's really making shopping an enjoyable experience!* And I might mirror their mood and become that happy shopper for some-one else.

We're connected in ways we can and can't see; kindness is one of these connections, and it impacts all of us – one way or another.

So I've become aware of kindnesses in my actions and in my attitude. I'm not saying that I'm kind all the time (because I'm a human being), but a small kindness goes a long way.

I am a person who wants to spread kindness; it's something I've realized is important to me. If a virus can cover the globe in just three months when people are trying to avoid it, imagine how fast kindness would spread if people are *not* trying to avoid it! This is why kindness is very important to me, and something I value within myself.

Another quality I've observed in myself is compassion. I don't know what other people are going through, why somebody is responding to me the way that they are. I may come up to somebody and say, "Hey, don't you just love the sunshine?" And they may respond with a *get out of my face* kind of energy. At that point, it would be up to me to choose how to respond to them.

I could react to what they said out of my own context (in which the sunshine is a good thing), or I can take a minute to think about their context – what pain might they be sitting in or what trial might they be going through right now? Instead of getting mad and returning rudeness for perceived rudeness, I can choose to have compassion for them.

If somebody doesn't think or believe the way I do about something, rather than arguing about who's right and who's wrong, what if I ask them what brought them to that belief? Why do they believe it? I'm sure there's a story there. So I've learned that compassion is another core value for me; I can see that it has changed how I move through the world and interact with everyone and everything in it.

I've also observed gratitude bubbling up in me. Or, rather, a different kind of gratitude has been revealing itself ...

Losing someone, or something, brings about another dimension of appreciation for their presence. But here's the thing – I don't have to wait until they're gone to be grateful for them, or to express that gratitude.

I've heard this many times before, but I didn't experience this kind of gratitude until after Rod died. Learning to see the things and people in my life now and being grateful for them *while I still have them* is another very important thing to me.

As a child, when I received a gift, I was taught to say, "Thank you." I was told I should be grateful for what I had and, in some situations, if that gratitude was not demonstrated, my parents might take that gift away from me. It's the idea that if I'm not going to be grateful for something, then I don't deserve to have it.

This idea was carried over into my adulthood. Somewhere along the way, I adopted that belief that if I'm not grateful for something – anything – God will take it away from me. As a result of this belief, I learned to search out everything in my life that I don't want to lose and to actively be grateful for it.

For example, I'm grateful that my car starts every morning. But I realized that underlying that gratitude is the idea that if I'm not grateful for my car, it will be taken away from me – it will break down, I will get in an accident, or it'll get stolen or whatever. One way or another, it will be taken from me.

This kind of gratitude believes that expressing gratitude for things (or people) will ensure their continuance in my life. But it is actually a fear-based attempt to stop the other shoe from dropping, so to speak, to stave off suffering. It comes from a scarcity mindset.

It's the idea that if I'm not grateful for something, it'll be taken away and I will be lacking something I think I need. But if I *am* grateful for it, I will get to keep it. And I want to keep it because I don't know if I'll be able to replace it once it's gone, and *then* I will be lacking something I need. It's gratitude with a "so that ..." attached to it.

This conditional gratitude takes me out of the present moment, bringing my focus to a future where I may or may not have something I think I need. This "Thank you" is followed by an ellipsis, or maybe even a question mark; a waiting or anticipation for what the outcome of this gratitude will be – wondering if I expressed my gratitude soon enough or if it was sincere enough for me to keep the thing.

So if my car starts right up again the next time, there's a sense of relief in knowing that it *was* enough. I think, *Whew! Looks like I was grateful enough last time. I hope my gratitude this time will be enough for her to start right up next time.* That's so stressful when I think about it now.

Living in this kind of gratitude left me wondering if Rod was taken away from me because my gratitude wasn't ... enough.

One spring, we had a family of mockingbirds nesting in the pear tree in our back yard. Once the nestlings were big enough to start trying out their wings, one baby bird flew down and was sitting in the sunshine in the grass not far from the tree where its nest was. It was being very still and quiet as it waited for its mama to come with food. But once she was in range, all efforts to remain invisible to prey were abandoned. That baby bird got so loud, and its gaping mouth bigger than its whole head! Mama arrived and put some food into her baby's mouth. When she left again to go forage for more food, the baby once again got still and quiet. Have you seen this? But when the mama comes back, the baby bird, still sitting there waiting, opens his mouth and screams once again until the mama puts more food in its waiting mouth.

That's a good illustration of what gratitude had been for me. Wherever I was, I trusted God to come to me, to provide for me; I sat still in anticipation of God coming to me to give me what I needed, like that baby bird waited for its mother. I believed that as long as I was grateful enough, God would continue to provide for me, and He wouldn't take away what has already been given. But if I wasn't grateful, He might not come back, and what I do have will eventually run out. This goes along with the fear-based idea of gratitude that I'd held.

On another occasion, I was watching the bees in my yard ...

There are different kinds of flowers in different places in my yard where bees can eat and gather pollen. It's like God is saying to the bees, "Here is a whole field. I have already provided for you abundantly – it's all already there, ready for the taking." All the bee has to do is decide which flower she's going to visit next! She will never run out of provision because even if that one bee eats everything in that one yard or in that one field, guess what? There's another yard, another field, and there's more flowers! She doesn't have to wait for – or even ask – God to bring her food because everything she needs *has already been provided* for her. And that bee will never run out of resources because God has already provided abundantly for that bee. The bee has only to see it.

What I came to understand is that gratitude reveals the abundance that God has *already provided.* It's not simply counting my blessings or naming things I am grateful for (aka those things I don't want to lose); it's that having a grateful heart reveals the abundance I am literally sitting in. Living in this kind of gratitude, from a mindset of abundance, is a whole different way of moving through life. Just like fear-based gratitude (or a scarcity mindset) blinds me to God's abundant provision, this kind of gratitude reveals it to me.

Being aware of the abundance and provision that is literally all around me all the time allows me to stay present in the moment, to be grateful for something or someone *while I still have them* without being concerned or distracted by an uncertain future.

This kind of "Thank you" is followed by a period. It's a statement of my present mindset without concern for what may follow. It's an acknowledgement that this thing or person exists in this moment. I can be grateful my car started right up this time and can get me to where I'm going. Period. No condition or expectation, no projecting into the future – positively or negatively.

It allows me to say, *"Today I am well. Today I am provided for. Come what may, right now I see and acknowledge the provision that is before me, and I am grateful for it.* Instead of a sigh of relief, there's a feeling of contentment.

Being able to be present with what is, allows me to more fully engage with what or who I am with, to be more focused on and just enjoy it or them.

I'm still observing myself and I'm still learning, but I can see as I continue to move forward in these values that they will shape the way I think and determine the things I do.

These values are not new to me; I believe they have been with me for a long time. But they were running in the background within the context and the confines of the pre-determined role/identity from which I had been operating. The foundation of that identity was the script – the social expectations and biblical interpretations of what it meant to be a woman and how to be a wife.

For example, let's take the golden rule – "Do unto others as you would have them do unto you." In this little saying, kindness is expressed *as it is relative to my own desire to receive it.* The kindness I would have expressed would have been based on the kindness that I wanted to receive; I wasn't kind for kindness's sake, but for my own comfort and benefit.

Similarly, my compassion would have expressed itself through the lens of my own lived experience rather than the lens of humanness; it could only extend as far as my context would allow it to. Within the confines of my old identity, instead of compassion, I might feel pity (or disgust, or con-fusion, etc.) if I couldn't understand or connect to someone else's situation.

And my gratitude, which was based on a scarcity mindset, was for self-preservation. It was limited to things and people within the context of my own existence. In addition, this kind of gratitude is focused on what *I believe* I need. If I don't believe that I need something – or someone – in my life, then there is no reason for me to be grateful for it, or for them. In fact, I might find myself glad to be rid of it rather than being grateful simply because it exists.

What's new about these values is that they are no longer running in the background being defined by something external to me; they are becoming the foundation for things that are defining my emerging identity. They are no longer operating within the confines of a predetermined anything; these values are becoming the baseline for my actions and my thoughts rather than being situational or conditioned upon the context of a predefined role or identity. These values now have free reign to express in ways that were not available to me in my previous context.

The way I see them now, these values are based simply on being a human being, of being a created thing like every other thing on this earth is a created thing. They are able to express in a much broader sense now – a sense of otherness – with a human-centric perspective rather than a "Gail-centric" or role- or expectation-centric perspective.

I am learning that values are neither feminine or masculine; they belong to every person regardless of gender or role. And these values I've observed in myself are relevant to all aspects of who I am. This perspective has helped me greatly in forming a new identity.

As that new identity takes shape, I am beginning to understand that having a sole identity as wife/woman was not incorrect; it was incomplete. I am more than the role I play or the body I walk around in. Neither Wife nor Woman represents a complete picture of who I am, but they are both part of what makes me, me.

I'm discovering that I am more than I have ever known (or allowed) myself to believe that I am, and I am just now beginning to explore that moreness.

Much in the same way that I am discovering that I am more than my gender – that my gender, my role, are only aspects of a larger identity – I have also been discovering that God is more than who I thought Him to be.

I had known God in a particular way, in a particular role of His own. I had identified Him through particular teachings, and when my lived experience no longer lined up with what I'd learned, I went on a journey seeking to know God as He truly is. Much like I was realizing about my own role and gender, I was coming to understand that most of what I knew about God and the role He plays in my life was not incorrect; it was incomplete.

I have been discovering a Creator that is so much more than what I have learned or experienced before. Some things I believed about Him before I now hold in a different context, and some things to a greater context.

And if I believe that I am created in His image, it should not surprise me to discover that I, too, am more than I think I am.

Looking back, I can see where my new identity timidly slipped into my lived experience before I was aware of its existence.

About four years after Rod died, I moved my parents from California to an assisted living facility close to my home in

Texas. My dad's health was declining beyond what his wife could handle, and this move was the best option for his care and for her well-being.

At the entrance of their building, there was a small lobby with seating for the residents. All visitors were required to sign in and out at the front desk/nurses station. Residents would gather in that seating area – some to be supervised, some for company. There wasn't always conversation or inter-action, but there was presence; they would come and sit with each other and know they were not alone.

One day after visiting with my parents, as I approached the lobby. I saw a few people gathered there, but it was quiet and quite somber. Seeing this, I decided I needed to change my energy, to adapt my mood to match theirs. There's an understanding – an unspoken script – that says because they're my elders, there is a prescribed manner in which I am to behave around them. So I slowed my pace and smoothed the bounce in my step, and I hid my smile.

Realizing I'd spent most of my life being who others expected me to be, I decided to go off-script this time. In-stead of changing my energy, I allowed my budding identity to determine my actions. So I smiled and bounced up to the desk, chatted with the nurse behind the counter as I signed out, then I headed to the door. I was carrying a box in my hands, so I turned around to push the door open with my back, still smiling.

With my back to the door, looking into the lobby, you know what I saw? Every person sitting in that reception area seemed a little lighter. Some of them were even smiling back at me.I didn't interact with any of them, only the nurse behind the desk. I just maintained my own energy, and I brought that with me into that space. And everyone was visibly affected by it.

Walking into the space like that showed me something about myself I'd never seen before. I was like a new little stem popping up through the soil unexpectedly, and I was curious about it. I was clearly aware that people's energy affects me because I felt my own energy changing as I approached the lobby. But this was the first time I got to see that I am not only affected by others, but I can also affect others.

This experience was my first evidence that a new identity was beginning to form. I couldn't identify it as that at the time, but moving in my own energy instead of adapting to the energies around me is something I have been observing since then, and I have consciously chosen to continue to explore.

7

Finding Me

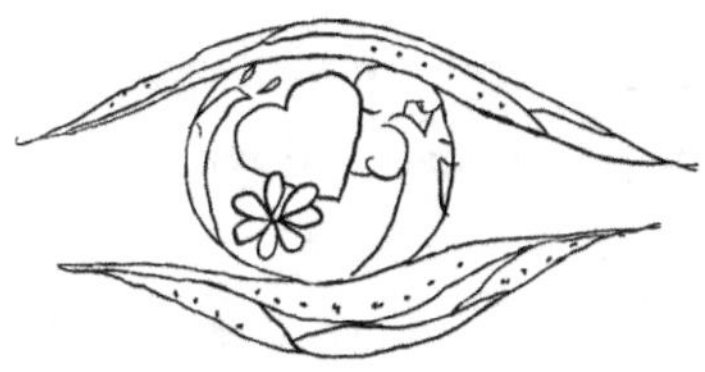

I began my search to find Me by exploring different things, remembering things I used to like, and trying things I've never been brave enough – or had opportunity – to try before.

Reading is one of the things I explored, even though reading and I had quite the history.

I never enjoyed reading for reading's sake. I mean, I read in high school and college because I had to, but even then I cheated, but not in the way you're probably thinking. Let me explain.

I remember being assigned *The Good Earth* (Pearl S. Buck, 1931) for a book report in high school. It was kind of a big book (by my standards), and I did not want to read it! Not. At. All. I felt so defeated just looking at it. Nevertheless, the assignment was the assignment, so I devised a plan that would be the most efficient with the least amount of work to get it done and turned in on time.

I had learned that a well written paragraph has three parts: The topic sentence that introduces what will be addressed in the paragraph, the body that relays all the pertinent information that was referenced in the topic sentence, and the conclusion that summarizes the whole paragraph. So I figured if I read the first and last sentence of every paragraph, it should make the reading go faster, and I'd get enough info to write a decent paper. Yup, I'd read the whole book like that. So I got started.

I don't know if I got bored, overwhelmed or distracted, but I didn't get very far. I had to revise my reading plan twice, reading less each time, and I ended up writing a book report on a book I basically skimmed. Reading was such a chore!

And that attitude towards reading stayed with me. If it's not assigned or relevant to information I'm looking for, It's not likely that I'll be reading it.

Despite my aversion to reading, when homeschooling my daughter, I ended up choosing literature-based curricula from second grade through high school graduation.

I started homeschooling Kristyn in first grade. Since we were planning on enrolling her in a private school for second grade, we chose the home version of the same curriculum the school used for first grade. But when it came time to enroll her for second grade, she was so distraught! She loved homeschooling and begged to continue. Not that we allowed the six-year-old to make the final decision, but we decided that her input on her education – at any age – should be a factor in our decision. And Rod and I decided to continue to homeschool her.

Without the pressure of having to fit into a second grade classroom, I had the opportunity to re-evaluate our curriculum choice, and were we both glad for this! While the curriculum we were using had a proven track record in the classroom, the home version did not seem a good fit for us.

And so began our adventures in literature-based curricula.

To be clear, I didn't choose them because they were literature-based; they fit her learning style and I liked the teaching methods they used.

Up until tenth grade, all of her curricula had books that I'd read with (if not aloud to) her, and I found myself actually enjoying reading for the first time as far as I could recall.

When I was no longer involved with her reading, I tried to keep reading just for myself, but it wasn't long before it once again felt like a chore. And I found myself not reading for pleasure once again.

Fast forward to about five years after Rod died. I had finally accepted that life was different for me now, and that I actually had the option to choose what I wanted to do with myself. As I pondered this new freedom, I remembered that I actually did enjoy reading at one time, and I actually missed it when I stopped. So I decided to give reading another go.

I didn't want to buy a book because I didn't know what I wanted to read. What if I bought a book and I didn't like it? So I went to the library. If I checked out a book and I didn't like it, I haven't lost anything but time.

I found myself wandering the aisles of the library. I had no idea what I was looking for, no idea what I liked to read. Do I like nonfiction or fiction? History or romance? Crime drama or self-help?

Rod was a voracious reader! At any given time, he was reading a nonfiction and a fiction book, and probably more than just those two. As I was walking through the library, I saw a particular author's name, and I remembered that Rod read that author. Or I recognized a title I knew that Rod had read before.

The thing is, I walked through this library, up and down the aisles, pointing out books that Rod either had read or would probably like to read, but clueless as to what I wanted to read. I knew Rod's reading tastes better than I knew my own! I literally had no idea where to start. I couldn't even decide whether I'd want to read fiction or nonfiction.

As tears welled up in my eyes, I remembered that the books I enjoyed reading to my daughter when we were homeschooling were mostly historical fiction, so I decided to look for those. But our community library is small, so there's not a separate section for historical fiction. I thought about searching the computer catalog, but I didn't know any author names or book titles to search for. (In my lostness, it didn't even occur to me to search by genre.)

So I just walked up and down the aisles, reading titles and looking at covers through tearfilled eyes. One book caught my attention, so I pulled it out to read the back. It was called *Life's Golden Ticket: A Story About Second Chances* (Brendan Bruchard, 2008) Never heard of the guy, never heard of the book, but a book about second chances sounded interesting.

So I checked it out. I loved it so much I ended up buying a copy!

This really sparked hope in me that there were books out there that I might actually want to read. I leaned more towards the self-help/personal growth genres at first. Some of them were able to put words to what I was experiencing. I could relate to those stories, and they expressed principles that I could apply to my own journey. But reading was still hit and miss for a while as I just didn't have space built into my days to accommodate it.

In 2021 I decided to be more intentional, and I set a reading goal for the year – 12 books. And I joined an online book club. I thought this would help me with any lingering decision paralysis when it came to choosing a book – there are so many to choose from – and knowing I'd be discussing it with others would help keep it on my radar. Well, the first book was all I needed to get me going – I was off and running on my own after that! I continued in the self-help/personal growth genre through the rest of the year, but I also sprinkled in a couple philosophy and theology books, and I read a total of eight books that year. Not the 12 I'd set as my goal, but definitely eight more than I would have read otherwise.

The next year I set my goal once again to 12 books. I threw in a couple of fiction books I remember having an interest in at some point in my life but just never got around to reading – or finishing reading. By the end of the year I read 13 books.

In 2023 I kept to my goal of 12 books, and actually read eight – including two in a fantasy series (in which each book has 1200-1300+ pages) and a murder mystery. But more importantly I continued to explore my taste and expand my repertoire.

I've surprised myself with some of my choices. I used to think some of the genres would have been too heady for me, and others the spine was too thick for me to even pick up.

As I look back over my lifelong on-and-off relationship with reading, I've made some observations.

Reading had been a utilitarian task for education or information purposes only, not for enjoyment. Perhaps this came about because I wasn't allowed recreational reading as a child until my homework and chores were done, and I carried this mindset into my adult life.

With a husband, three kids, a job, and a home, my chores were never done. When reading became a chore of sorts while homeschooling, something I was required to do for some reason other than recreation, I was able to read guilt-free (so to speak). But when that season was over, reading once again became elusive.

It wasn't until my time became my own – without the demands of husband and kids – that I even began to think about making time to read.

Something else I explored was art.

I'd never considered myself to be an artistic person. I was creative, but I needed a pattern or template to work from. I considered myself a better copycat than an artist.

I learned to sew and crochet as a child (with two grandmothers and a mom to teach me, it was inevitable!). For years when my kids were growing up I created scrapbooks of our family photos, recording our life together. I loved to cross-stitch and I've crocheted and sewn many things over the years.

Much like reading, all of my creating was utilitarian – for either my personal for family use, for a gift, for display or decor, or for sale. If I didn't have one of these reasons for me to create something, I wouldn't make it.

When I learned to crochet dish rags, I made a good number of them for my own kitchen, gave some away, and put some in my shop. But my kitchen drawers could only hold so many, and I only have so many friends who want them, and I didn't have space for a large inventory for my shop, so I stopped making them. I stopped creating.

One day I had a new thought about art – what if the purpose of the art was the making of it? Art for the sake of art. Kids do this all the time – just make stuff because they want to! What if I could create something in the same way? If its purpose was simply to be made, then, having achieved its purpose, it could be discarded.

WHAAAT?!? *Throw art away?* Really it was more like *Throw away perfectly good resources?* It was unthinkable, wasteful, and poor stewardship!

But I decided to ignore those old voices in my head. I can't explore something new if I keep listening to the old voices. So I bought a paint-by-number set – something I totally enjoyed as a kid (and still have two puppy dogs I painted way back when) – with the intention of painting them then throwing them in the trash.

It felt rebellious. It felt irresponsible. And it was freeing. I could paint because I wanted to paint. That was it.

Art for the sake of art.

Suddenly, I saw creation differently – nature, stars, bugs, trees. I wondered if God created what he did simply because he wanted to. Not as gifts or tools, not for show or profit.

By allowing myself to explore this possibility, I have discovered that I like to doodle. I have several small sketchbooks (including a few I've made myself from printer paper and scrapbook paper I managed to hang onto when I stopped scrapbooking because everything went digital) full of doodles. Sometimes I still take inspiration from other doodlers, but either way I doodle for no other reason than because I want to.

And I love having that creative outlet available to me at any time, not just when it's utilitarian or for some larger purpose.

I began to come out of that unknowing of who I am by choosing to explore different things. These are just a couple of examples.

I continue to find Me whenever I find something that makes me smile or brings me joy. I've been discovering my own creativity by being open to new things or, in some cases, remembering old things.

And, in case you're wondering, I have gone back and re-read *The Good Earth*. Properly. And it made me cry.

8

Widow

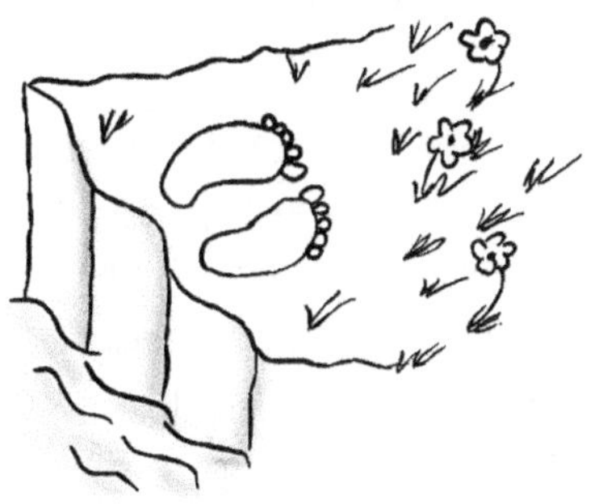

I was not old when Rod died; I was 51. We became grand-parents at 48. Our youngest child had just started college when we were 50. I did not know how to be a widow at all, much less at 51, with a kid in college and two young grandbabies. I couldn't even say the W-word, let alone be one.

If I live to be as old as my Grama, I could be a widow for almost 40 years – that's like another lifetime – and longer than Rod and I even knew each other!

I *couldn't* accept that I was a widow at this age.

I'd spent most of my life (if not all of it) following somebody else's script and being someone else's somebody – Bob's daughter, Rod's wife, my kids' mom. But this widow thing, happening at this stage of my life leaves me in a place that doesn't make me anybody's anything. It's just me, a widow.

But what does Widow do, where is her place in the world, and what is her purpose? It's not a common topic of conversation. I don't know many songs about Widow or being widowed. And in TV shows where I've actually seen Widow, she's not usually a regular character, and she's generally ignored or dismissed, or even forgotten. Or at least the idea of her being a widow is.

There were no clear-cut answers out there for Widow, which is odd considering the very specific expectations placed on Wife and Woman when I was growing up. (Not to mention the statistical data that shows 75% of married women out-live their husbands.) I certainly didn't like the Widow options offered by our American culture.

Our culture casts Widow as a white haired elderly woman living in the same house that Wife lived in, with all the furniture and decor remaining exactly as Wife had them. She lives alone pining for Husband, biding her time until she joins him in bliss. Or finds a new husband.

Is this to be the rest of my life? Is this who Widow Gail is expected to be?!

Oh, *hell*, no!

If I must be a widow, I refuse to follow these cultural expectations based on our current social norms. I followed a script before, and I lost Me in the process. I will not do that again.

So, here I am. A Widow, going off-script with very few resources to draw on for guidance or direction.

My dad was widowed in his early 40s, but I was 12 so I had no clue what it was like for him. I was just trying to get through puberty without a mom.

He remarried four years after my mom died. His new wife was a widow but that didn't seem to be part of her life; it was just something that happened to her once. She was married to my dad now, and she rarely talked about her late husband. Or my mom.

Two other widows in my life were my Grama (my father's mother) and my Nana (my mother's mother). My Grama lived as a widow for nearly 30 years. I saw her living independently, taking care of herself and her own affairs until just a few months before she died at 88. But I also saw the despair my Nana experienced after my Popi died.

My Grama became a widow when she was 59 years old. I don't remember my grandfather at all; I was four and a half when he died. I never saw my Grama as a widow; she was just my Grama.

As I got older, and started to ask her quesitons about my grandfather, she would tell me things about him and about their relationship that maybe she didn't appreciate, or things he did that she did not prefer, but I don't ever remember her saying anything negative about him. She never diminished him as a person or as a husband, or put him in a bad light.

She was one of those little blue-haired old ladies. From my earliest memories, she had short, white hair that was wavy, like the finger waves she wore as a young woman in the 1920s.

I remember she had this big gray bottle of hair rinse with a little pink pop-up spout. After she washed her hair, she would lean over the bathroom sink with a towel around her shoulders and squeeze this blue liquid all over her head until her hair was saturated. She told me she used this rinse because her white hair would take on a dingy yellow look, and the blue rinse helped keep it looking silver-white. She was pretty good about knowing how much to use but there were those times that she used a little too much, and it gave her hair a bluish tint.

I never thought of her as a single woman when I was younger, but having figured out for herself how to live on her own for nearly 30 years after my grandfather died is pretty amazing. She paid her bills, took her meds, lived in her own mobile home in a mobile home park, and walked everywhere or took a bus to get wherever she wanted to go. All 4'11" of her stood straight with square shoulders, and her mind was sharp until the day she died. She was pretty badass for being widowed in the 1960s when the prevailing norm was that a woman's value was wrapped up in her husband.

Life was very different for my Nana after my Popi died. She was in her late 60s when he died. I was 18, so I definitely have memories of Popi, and of the two of them together.

They entertained neighbors, hosted parties, and traveled to Spain for a few weeks every summer. Nana was a lady (with actual royalty in her lineage!), always gracious and hospitable.

The only time I remember seeing her not dressed for the day – including hair, makeup and accessories – was when I spent the night at her house. Even then, most mornings she was up and at least dressed before I was awake. She was always ready for whatever goings-on were on tap for the day, and there always seemed to be goings-on.

After Popi died she'd sit on her couch all day without even as much as running a brush through her hair – which was, much to my dismay, starting to show white roots. That's when I realized that she'd been coloring her hair for my whole lifetime – at least! In my 18 years knowing her, I never saw the woman with anything other than brown hair. Never. Not once.

She wasn't interested in going anywhere or seeing anyone, or even leaving the house. Her smile was ... how can I describe her smile in those days? It was just sad, like an echo of a smile. It was a smile that remembered that there had once been joy in her life, a joy she just couldn't find any more. I watched her begin to wither away, without any effort or even desire to go on. She just didn't care. I don't know if she ever left the house or if she was eating regularly. I don't even know if she was taking care of their poodle, Nicky.

One day, in the middle of the day, I went to visit my Nana unannounced. As I pulled up, I could see from the driveway that the curtains in the living room window were still closed. That was unusual because she used to open them every morning, filling the room with light. Always.

I went into her house, and she was sitting on the couch in the dark. The couch was positioned right under that big window I saw from the driveway. With all the trees in their front yard, the view out of the window was like a huge wall painting when the curtains were pulled back. She smiled that sad smile and greeted me. I don't remember if she got up, or if I just sat down beside her.

She was just sitting in that dark living room, no lights on, not even the TV. She was still in her pajamas and bathrobe. She was just sitting there, staring into a dark, silent room. I opened the curtains for her while I was there, though she hardly seemed to notice.

Eight months after my Popi died, she remarried. Her new husband had been married to one of her sisters who had died a number of years before; being widowed himself, he had been living on his own.

After they married, I watched my Nana come back to life! She was once again dressed to the nines and ready for anything, makeup and accessories perfect, and her hair a single shade of brown once again. They started traveling like she used to do with Popi, and she was a social butterfly again. She found her joy, and with it she found her smile.

A lot of the family didn't like that they married (which isn't that uncommon for the family of the widow, even now). I don't know if they were upset at Nana for remarrying so soon, or if they were mad because of who she married. But it didn't seem to matter to either my Nana or her new husband.

I found out much later the story behind them getting married. My Popi had lung cancer. Before he died – knowing that he was going to die, and knowing his wife – he asked his widowed brother-in-law to marry his wife. Popi knew she'd need someone to take care of her. So it turns out that he was simply honoring my Popi's request. I thought that was a beautiful demonstration of my Popi's love for my Nana, even after his death.

Nana and her new husband were married for 10 years before Nana passed away, and he died about three months later. But from what I saw, I think if she hadn't remarried, she'd have been dead within a year of Popi's death.

Even though I knew both of my grandmothers had lost their husbands, I never thought of them as widows. Grama was just my grandmother without a grandfather. I knew Nana was sad about losing Popi, but that seemed to fade away after she remarried and her life returned to the way it had been before. They were just my grandmothers living their lives the best way they knew how.

After Rod died, I was able to see them both differently. Even though they have both been gone for some time, I can see now how their life choices may have been informed by their losses. They were both processing their grief and figuring out how to exist in a world without their husbands. My Grama figured out how to live on her own, and took care of herself for three decades. My Nana remarried to save her life, and she found new joy there.

Since I didn't see them as widows at the time of Rod's death, I didn't look to them as resources to guide or inspire me, so their experiences as widows didn't have a conscious impact on what my version of widowhood would look like. I was pretty much left to my own devices to figure this widow thing out.

Once I was able to admit to myself that I was really and truly a widow, I made a couple of decisions about what that would look like for me. Actually, they were declarations of what Widow would NOT look like for me.

Deciding what Widow would NOT look like for me was like digging up and hauling away any expectations I may have had about widowhood. Only then could I go off-script to discover what I wanted Widow to mean for me.

First and foremost, I was not going to walk around dressed in black and be sad all the time. Secondly, I decided that I never want to get to a point where I am not sad about Rod dying.

My intention with my first decision was that I was not going to mope around with a dark cloud hanging over my head all the time making everyone uncomfortable, feeling like they have to walk on eggshells around me. I was not going to lose sight of the good things in life, even if it meant simply acknowledging their existence when I couldn't be grateful.

I was basically refusing to let my grief overshadow every other aspect of my being, or to let it define my existence. I was somehow going to find joy again, though at first I had no idea if that was actually possible.

My second decision sounds like I'm saying that I always want to be sad. But that is exactly what my first declaration was determined to avoid!

I believed that if I were to look back on my years and experiences with Rod and not feel some kind or amount of sadness, that would somehow diminish or dismiss those memories or experiences we shared. We're usually sad when something fun or enjoyable concludes – like when your vacation is over, or you finish watching a favorite movie. If I'm not sad in those times, I might wonder if I truly enjoyed those things.

If I was ever not sad about losing Rod, I believed it would mean that I didn't really love him, or that the experiences we shared and the years I spent with him didn't matter; that my memories of him and the things we shared weren't really all that important to me. Well, not important enough for me to be sad about them being over, anyway.

My memories are the only things I have left of him; I couldn't bear dismissing or losing those, too. So I decided that the best way to hang on to those memories would be to always be at least a little bit sad that they were over.

But this sadness wouldn't permeate my whole life, being that dark cloud always following me around (thus violating my first declaration). It would remain mostly in quiet moments, just to myself. Silent tears seeing an older couple holding hands. Ugly-crying alone in the car when our song came on. Tears mingling with the laughter of a funny story being told. This type of sadness would be specific and mostly private.

I just couldn't bear to think that I would ever get to a place where his importance, his very presence in my life, didn't seem to matter. I couldn't dare imagine a time that I would ever be able to just say, *Well, that was fun. What's next?*

But in the process of healing and growing, I've learned that sadness doesn't have to be part of my memories. Feeling sadness – or not – is not an indication of importance, or lack thereof, of whether or not I loved Rod or valued the experiences we shared. Those things are important because they are part of my life. They brought joy and added something good to my existence. I can remember all those years, all the things we shared, with joy and fondness without diminishing their importance or impact; sadness does not have to be part of that equation, though it certainly can be. The important thing is that I remember. How I feel when I do is up to me.

In hindsight, I can see how both of these decisions may have been influenced on a subconscious level by my grand-mothers' experiences. It wasn't until I was well into my own widow journey that I reflected back on what I knew of their experiences and saw the patterns that likely had some un-conscious impact on my own journey.

My refusal to be the 'grieving widow' could have been inspired by my Nana. It was difficult for me to see her that way, and I didn't want to put my loved ones through that. It could be that I was so adamant about this because I perceived that my relationship with Rod was similar to her relationship with Popi, and I could see myself going down the same road she did.

I also never wanted to become so independent that Rod would become a side note in my life. I can't say my Grama was never sad; what I do remember were matter-of-fact stories she told about my grandpa right there next to stories of when she worked in the garment district making lingerie in 1920s New York. I can see how this could have been a reflection of my Grama's relationship with my grandpa; she wasn't always happy in her marriage, so I wonder how that might have played into her building a new life on her own after his passing.

Once I started digging up and identifying all the perceived "rules" and expectations I held about widowhood and got past what Widow would NOT look like for me, I was able to decide for myself what it might look like for me.

As I began exploring who I wanted Widow Gail to be, I allowed *myself* – not culture – to decide what else it might look like. Here are some of the things I have included in my experience as a widow:

- *Student.* I completed two years at community college and got a Certificate in Interpreting for the Deaf. I must've looked funny to the other students; I'm sure they didn't have a grandma in too many of their classes!

- *Realtor.* Well, I didn't become one, but I hired one and sold our house of 23 years and bought my own house only ten months after Rod died. (I'll talk more about making big decisions in the first year in Chapter 26.)

- *Seamstress.* I got out my 30+ year old Singer Touch-N-Sew sewing machine and opened an Etsy shop. I sewed some stuff, and I made a little money.

- *Life Coach for Widows.* I found that I was "uniquely qualified to minister to a whole new set of people." Rod said this of himself not long after he was diagnosed with cancer. I am happy to have something from him that I could hang on to that still encourages and empowers me.

- *Writer.* As my story unfolded, I realized that sharing my experience might help other widows feel not so alone. Or at least not as crazy.

And I was the one who decided to do (and to stop doing) all these things on my own. I signed myself up for school, and I contacted the realtor. I opened my Etsy shop, and I signed up for the Life Coaching course. And I decided to write this book.

As I observed myself in each of these activities (oddly in about two-year increments), I saw a person making decisions – for better or worse – without having to check in with anyone. A person willing to try new things with or without anyone's input or approval. A person capable of stepping out on her own, learning that she doesn't have to wait for permission or someone else to take the lead, or even need anyone to go with her.

I began to see who I am outside of external expectations.

These were hard decisions that seemed to push Rod to the periphery of my life, and I didn't like that at all. I remember fighting back tears as I walked to my classes, or sat out in the car between classes just bawling. I didn't like the fact that I *could* be at school (meaning that no one else needed me to do anything or be anywhere for them). And I hated *why* I could be there – the reason I could quit my job and pursue this course of action at all was *because* Rod died.

So at first, I didn't like this new Widow me that was emerging. But the more things I did – and continue to do – on my own, the more confidence I gained in myself. The tearful realization that I no longer had to check in with anyone necessitated that I check in with myself, and waiting for external approval that just wasn't coming taught me to look for that approval within myself. Learning how to be there for myself demonstrated to me that I actually could survive – even thrive – after Rod.

Over time, I actually began to admire my new bad-ass widow self.

But even Widow is not a complete identity, it is simply another aspect of who I am.

9

Single: A Different Kind of Woman

The place I would traditionally look to for direction (my church) didn't talk much about the role of single women, so I didn't find much guidance there on how to live on my own in the long term. I had heard general teachings on how the church was to take care of widows, but not many directly to the widow herself on how she should live. And most of what I learned about single women from the church was only applicable until she *found* a husband. But any teachings on how a woman is to move forward *without* a husband? Yeah, those were few and far between, and usually came with 'special circumstances.' Nevertheless, I'm learning a lot about what it looks like to be a single woman in the US in the 21st century.

Before widowhood launched me into the single life, whenever my single friends shared with me what some of their challenges were, I would acknowledge them and try to help if I could. But I lacked the context to fully empathize with their struggles.

For example, if a single friend shared an encounter she had with a man where she spoke up for herself and got what she needed (and I could see how proud she was that it worked), I didn't think too much about it. I'm a woman, and I almost always got what I needed, so that seemed normal to me. But, you see, if I had an encounter with a man that didn't go the way I thought it should, I called Rod. He'd speak Man to the man, and the thing would get resolved and that's how I'd get what I needed. I spoke up for myself, too, but was only heard to a point. Beyond that, my voice was heard through Rod. I didn't see it as a huge deal when a single woman's voice was heard by a man because I was not focusing on *how* my voice was heard, just *that* it was heard. Ultimately, looking back on it now, I realize it wasn't my voice that was being heard at all – men were responding to Rod's.

Now I realize without that interpreter to back me up, my voice often gets dismissed. And for me to stand up for myself and make my own voice be heard is a challenging task. So now when I hear of a single woman – any woman, really – in an encounter with a man and she tells how she stood her ground, made a decision, and he abided by it, she's a hero to me!

As much as I'd like to be like these brave, bold women, I still fall back into that role that puts me on a lower rung in the hierarchy, in a place of submission as a woman, a place I have lived in for most of my life.

The idea that a man is intrinsically smarter or somehow more capable than I am – the thought that his words are more important than or take precedence over mine – is completely arbitrary to me now.

I believe a man and a woman are both expressions and reflections of God. He said that we are equal, that we, as human beings, are the same in priority, in importance, and in value. Yet we live within a hierarchy, a man-made system of roles based on gender. I somehow managed to live in this dichotomy that taught me that I am created equal in theory, but in practice I am something less.

This place of less value and of subordination in the greater society did not bother me too much – because of Rod. In our marriage, I knew I was valued. And while I was submissive to him as head of our household, he did not behave as my superior; we both understood that my submission to him as my husband was not a reflection of my personal value but a practical necessity in running a household and raising a family.

And now, without Rod, I am realizing that I never learned how to live into the equality that I was taught I had. I am still figuring out how to live within that socially constructed framework while also living as an equal.

During the pandemic and subsequent quarantine, I did a lot of self-exploration and self-examination. Without the constant presence of men in my day-to-day life, there was no one for me to be submissive to. I had time to breathe, so to speak, to experience the water I'm swimming in now. I had a sufficient break from those expectations to give myself the opportunity to think of myself as an equal in a practical sense.

It's like if you're standing outside in a storm, your concern is about the storm, not about staying dry. You know you're getting wet so there's no reason to try to stay dry; your focus is on staying safe.

It's not until you get out of the pouring rain that you then begin to think about getting out of wet clothes and finding something dry to put on, and grabbing a towel to dry your hair. It's coming in out of the rain that allows for the time and/or opportunity to undo what the rain has done.

Having a reprieve from directly and constantly experiencing male dominance in my life was like coming in out of the rain. I finally got to see what my new place *could* be, and to assess how I might step into that place of equality in the practical sense. I got to take off the social hierarchy for a bit and look for something different.

My search for that "something different" started by observing other women who have learned to navigate these waters. I got curious about what life might look like for me if I asserted myself, if I stood up for myself when encountering a man – or anyone, really – who might hold me to a place of less than.

As I observed these women, instead of dismissively thinking *that wasn't her place*, or *she's got a lot of nerve* like I used to think, I paid attention to her word choices, her posture, and body language – I started noticing *how* she did it.

I listened as they'd share experiences that were just normal everyday experiences for them, but I heard them very differently than I had heard before. I stopped focusing just on what they were doing, and started paying attention to the whole interaction. I was learning about the water they were swimming in, and I asked myself, *Could I be that resolute and confident? Could I swim in that water?*

I could feel sparks of confidence as I watched these women, and I started thinking, *I am worth listening to. I have ideas that are valid. I have thoughts that are important, and my words have value.*

It was like putting on dry clothes after being soaked by the rain.

But I also paid attention to how people around her responded, and I saw a dark side of being a strong, confident woman: our society does not look well on them. When she speaks her mind or achieves personal (or professional) success, she's called loud, pushy, or gets labeled a bitch. Or she gets accused of manipulating people or sleeping her way to success. If I move to a place of confidence where I'm able to live into my inherent value and my equality as a human being, am I willing to bear these labels?

These were definitely turbulent waters, quite different from the relatively calm waters that Wife swam in.

In December, 2020, I got the opportunity to take a dip in that water when I had a slab leak under my kitchen sink. All of a sudden I was dealing with a lot of men – plumbers, contractors, and all of the workers. I knew this was an opportunity for me to see if I had what it takes to be like the strong, confident women I'd been observing.

At first, I found it quite easy to express my preferences when the contractor made a suggestion and I had a different idea, or even to simply say "No" if he told me how things were going to go and I was not comfortable with his plan.

I actually spoke up for myself right from the beginning. He gave me his start date for the project, but I wanted to start the following week ... for reasons. He was pretty receptive, and said, "Okay, we'll start next week."

That gave me evidence that I actually can say something, and it will be respected rather than diminished, belittled, or contradicted. Awesome. So as this working relationship went on to get this project done, I continued to voice my ideas and opinions, and they were met *on the surface* with acknowledgement, with validation, and even with respect. So I thought *Okay, I can do this!* And things continued moving right along.

Or so it seemed.

While he agreed to whatever changes I was wanting to make, he let me know that implementing my changes was going to delay the completion of my project. Ok, fine.

But as the project progressed, he became less and less communicative with me. When he did respond to my texts, they were curt and dismissive. He often didn't answer my questions, only giving me the most minimal response he possibly could after repeated requests.

For example, I asked him specifically for a timeline and step-by-step outline of the project. All I knew at that point was that his crew was going to come into my home on a day for a few hours, do a thing and leave, then come back some days later when it was time for the next step and so on until the job was done. But I was going to have to live in this environment between the steps. I was the one that was going to be affected by not having access to my kitchen or laundry room until he decided to come back for the next step. What I needed was a daily schedule so I'd know how long I would be out of that part of the house so I could plan accordingly.

Instead of providing me with the project schedule as I requested, he said, "We'll be out on this day at this time to begin the project." Period. He gave no indication of how long they'd be here, or when they'd be back for the next step, so I still had no idea how long I would be out of my kitchen and without my washer and dryer, or how long I'd have to take my dog out the front door and walk her around the house into the back yard, since the only door to my backyard is in the kitchen.

Looking back, I can see how his response to me asserting myself was to ignore or delay me and to put other projects ahead of mine. It felt like I was being punished for not falling in line with his plan or following his lead, and then I was blamed for said delays.

Towards the end of the project I realized I was getting mad at things I couldn't control, so I started to look for the things I *could* control.

He had told me more than once that his crew would be at my house between 7:00 and 9:00 am to start work. I was up and dressed, and had all the pets tended to and contained by 7:00am. They didn't show up until after 9:00. On another day, it was almost 11:00.

I decided I couldn't control what time his crew got to my house, but I could control what time I let them into my house.

So when the contractor said his crew would be there between 7:00 and 9:00 for the next step of the job, I told him I'd be ready to let his crew in to start the work at 9:00am. Wouldn't you know it – his worker actually showed up at 8:00! He wasn't too happy about spending the next hour sitting in his truck.

I gotta say it felt pretty good to hold my boundary, to stay in control of what was mine to control. I did my regular morning routine without rushing, and the pets didn't have to be contained any longer than necessary for the work to get done. It was a much less stressful morning ... for me, anyway.

I'm pretty sure that if Rod were here, this project would have actually been finished in the expected two weeks instead of the four months it actually took.

Being a woman without a man is like swimming upstream, and these are not muscles I've had to use before now. This experience showed me where I had indeed made progress, and where I still have work to do to be heard and acknowledged as a woman in a man's world.

As my experience of being a single woman continues to change, I continue to learn how to live independently and progress towards wholeness. Consequently, how I view and understand marriage is also changing.

In a marriage, I'd want to be able to be myself, to maintain my own identity as an individual while being married. I would like to view myself and my partner as co-equals. I would want to do things for him because he is a human being who I care about, not because I am subordinate or because it's expected of me.

And I would want to know that he was also free to be himself with me, that he would likewise do things for me because he cared for me, not because of social (or even my lingering personal) expectations. I would want him to view me as a partner, not someone to be dominant over or to be dependent upon him.

Legally we would still be called husband and wife, and that title still carries all my previous experience and expectations with it. But relationally I am no longer willing to fulfill a role just because I'm a woman and it's my place. But without that role or hierarchy, I have yet to figure out how a marriage relationship differs from any other relationship between equals.

If I were to pursue a relationship again, I'd want to be my own person, not someone's wife. I'd want my interactions with this person to be based on my own values, preferences, and needs rather than making myself secondary or subject to him, or with his ideals and preferences as my default.

As I continue to discover myself and become my own person, I realize that I don't know how to reconcile an 'own person' with what I know Wife to be. How do you have a marriage with two independent and whole individuals?

I don't know the answer to that yet, but I feel like that's the kind of relationship I would want – one where I can be and operate from a place of being completely me while allowing my partner to do the same.

Here's an example of me operating from my individuality. For dinner one night, I was going to saute zucchini with onions and tomatoes. When I've made this before, my daughter said it smelled good and she would like to have some, but she chose not to because she doesn't like onions. When I was making it this time, she said would like to have some – sans the onions. I felt bad, like it was my fault she missed out. My first thought was to just leave them out, defaulting to her preferences because I want her to be able to enjoy the rest of the dish. But that made me a little sad because I wanted onions in it.

I could have stopped there, seeing her preference as more important than mine. And normally I would have deferred to her preference – or Rod's, or anyone else's really – and I would have eaten it without onions. That's what I'd always done.

I acknowledged that putting in onions would diminish *her* enjoyment of the meal. What I never really acknowledged before was that leaving them out would diminish *my* enjoyment of the dish.

So I thought about that for a minute. It occurred to me to saute the onions first and take them out of the pan before making the rest of the dish. Once everything was ready, I could add the sauteed onions to my own plate.

I'm learning to ask myself if there might be a way for us both to have our preferences met. In my example above, it was asking if there was a way for her to have this dish without onions AND for me to have it with onions. And the answer was yes, once I got out of the mindset that there were only two options.

When there's a conflict of preferences, I now realize it's neither necessary for nor required of me to give up my preference *so that* someone else can have theirs. I'm learning to not have my first reaction be to give up what I want in any given situation, but instead to look for option C.

So let's say, in the future, I decide to go to the movies with a partner. If our goal of going to the movies is to spend time with one another, then what's on the screen is secondary. We can go to any movie that sounds interesting and both still get what we want.

But what if the point was to see a particular movie, but we want to see different movies? Well, this would create a conflict for me. My default would have been to defer, even if that means me not getting to see the movie I wanted to see, and sitting through a movie I wasn't interested in seeing instead.

In learning to look for solutions outside of the 'this or that' thinking, I might ask myself, *How we might each get to see the movies we want to see?*

One solution might be that we find showtimes close to one another at the same theater, and each of us go to our respective screens. After both movies are over, we can go to dinner together and talk about our movies, right? This solution would accommodate both movie preferences.

It might be nice to have a partner like this, but it's not something I'm interested in pursuing at this point. I'm kinda enjoying being autonomous, learning to be my own complete person.

IO

Finding Wholeness

As I am becoming my own person, I am learning to be and to provide for myself everything that Rod was to me and did for me. **I am learning to find what I need within myself or from my own resources.**

This doesn't mean that I must do everything for or by myself, or that I don't need people in my life who will help from time to time. What it does mean is that I get to make decisions or choose how to solve problems based on my own experience and knowledge (and my ability to acquire it) instead of believing I am incapable based on an arbitrary set of expectations based on my gender and/or role.

Living into this idea of wholeness is proving to be a quite different experience for me. I lived my whole adult life believing that Wife without Husband is incomplete; she is *unable* to be complete on her own. And that a woman is just a wife who hasn't found a husband yet.

Husbands complete Wives, and Wives complete Husbands. The two shall become one; they are one flesh.

The implication here is that a woman without a husband is incomplete, as is a man without a wife. The desire is for completeness or wholeness; therefore, the desire is for Wife or Husband. But I was unaware of the flip-side of this ideology, that I, as an individual, am incomplete. That I need another person in order to *become* complete.

Looking back, I can see how Rod and I completed one another – in areas where Rod was weak, I was strong, and in areas where I was weak, he was strong. We complemented and completed one another in those ways.

But that mindset perpetuated our individual weaknesses because there was no need to improve them – we had each other to make up the deficit.

Here's an example.

Rod was an IT guy – he loved his gadgets. I'd even refer to his computers and gadgets as 'the other woman.' And he was good at what he did. Really good. Whenever I had a computer (or general electronics) problem, I'd bring it to him and it would be magically fixed. He even restored a bunch of photos I once permanently deleted by accident. (I guess it wasn't so permanent ... if you knew where to look.)

Early in our marriage, I would ask him to show me how to fix e-things, but he decided it would take more time for him to explain it to me than it would if he just did it himself, so he'd just fix it. I might have been able to figure it out for myself ... eventually ... but it was just more efficient (and easier for both of us) if I just brought it to him to fix.

After he died, I had a shouting match and tear-fest when I had to install a second cable box on my old tube TV by myself. And in one of my classes, it was all I could do to not break down in tears when we were told to create a Power-Point presentation in class (I'd never made a PowerPoint presentation before).

Here's another example ...

Rod's system of paying bills was the 'Lazy Susan' method, as he called it. That's where you put all the bills on a Lazy Susan, give it a spin, and pay whichever one(s) fly off. Or he'd pay a bill when they'd call for payment, or when the utilities got turned off. He was capable of managing our finances, he just didn't have the interest (or patience) to do it. So I did the budget and paid the bills. And because everything got paid on time, he never had to develop that skill (or patience).

I figured out a couple different ways I could deal with things (that Rod would have likely handled) as they came up.

Sometimes, I just figure stuff out and get it done.
When I recently switched my phone service from one provider to another, there were some unforeseen technical issues

that left me with a non-working phone number for three days while each provider insisted that the problem resided with the other provider. I was so frustrated with the whole situation!

When I finally got it resolved, my daughter told me she was proud of me! When I asked why, she noted that I didn't have the tech-crisis meltdown she's seen me have in the past. Oftentimes those meltdowns had less to do with the technology itself and everything to do with the fact that Rod wasn't there to fix it ... which then devolved into the sadness and pain of Rod not being here. But, this time, I was just able to do it.

On another occasion, I started a small load of laundry and set the water level accordingly. I noticed the tub was filling longer than it should have for a small load, so I checked it out. The tub was full to the brim, about to overflow – and still filling!

My first thought (after turning the washer to a drain and spin cycle) was wondering who I could call to fix this. It would probably be a $2 part and five minute repair that I'd have to pay a full service call for. *sigh* I ran through my budget in my head to figure out where these funds might come from – and when.

On the off-chance that I was right about the $2/five-minute repair, I went to my computer. Google gave me possible causes for this problem, and YouTube showed me how to fix it – and I fixed it!

I was right about the five minutes, but I didn't even need a part – a hose had come off; I just had to reconnect it. YouTube and Google have become valuable resources for me!

I didn't need to call a plumber that time, but I knew there would be times I would need help. So ...

Sometimes, I call in the experts.

I had an experience that prompted me to build a list of go-to folks for different jobs.

Several months after Rod died, I had to call a repair person to come fix the A/C in the house. Finding and scheduling a tech seemed very normal (as that responsibility had typically fallen to me since I was usually at home during the day) until I got the text that he was on his way.

Rod always knew when there was going to be someone in the house, and I knew that he could be home in a matter of minutes if I needed him to be. And if I wasn't able to reach him immediately in an emergency, I knew he'd be home in a matter of hours after work. I felt a wave of panic shoot right through me as I realized I was alone in the house, and I had no one to call if something untoward was to happen. And it could be days before anyone would find me if it did!

I remembered hearing that it's helpful for single women to turn on the shower while the repairman is in the house to give the illusion that someone else is home – so I decided to do that just as he arrived.

But what if it takes him longer to do the repair than a normal shower would last? I needed some other reassurance that I would be safe, so I called my son, Ryan, and asked if he'd call me while the repairman was at the house. I would pretend to be talking to Rod about after-work plans. (And I remembered to 'check' on the person taking a leisurely shower, and I turned off the water.)

As it turned out, everything was fine – there was no suspicious activity, and the A/C was back up and running by the time he left. But I didn't want to go through that every time I needed a professional to come to the house for some work.

To build my list, I looked at reviews as well as the experiences of other women to help me find folks I'd feel safe letting into my home when I was alone. In this way, I vetted a plumber, pest control guy, electrician, etc., as a need arose. I'd look for a professional who would respect me as an individual and treat me as an equal rather than a subordinate. But more important than that, I was looking for those with whom I could be fairly certain I would be safe, and who wouldn't take advantage of me being a single woman, or a widow. (Sadly, this does happen.) This was especially important to me if I was going to be alone in my house with a repairman.

Even with my list and my new-found confidence, sometimes I called in reinforcements simply because I didn't want to deal with it. The difference is now I know I'm capable of taking care of things myself. Asking for help in these instances is a choice, not a necessity. And that feels pretty good.

Rod and I not only filled in each other's weak spots in the area of skill sets or task distribution, but we also met each other's deeper personal needs. I was aware of some of those needs he met for me, but his absence revealed other needs that I was unaware of because he had been meeting them for me for so long. Suddenly not having a need met was like all the lights going off, or staring into the void from the edge of a cliff. With that awareness, I had to learn how to meet my own needs, even ones I've never had to think about before. These are some of the known and unknown needs I have learned to meet for myself.

Financial stability.

We became a one-income family about a year before Kristyn was born. Since that time, I'd work part-time off and on, but my income was usually extra spending money. Thankfully, Rod had life insurance that was enough for me to pay off all our debts (except the mortgage), and I invested the rest so that I could live on earned interest. I was advised that this was not a long-term solution, and that finding a job would be ideal – hence the return to college.

But even with that degree and certification, I realized that I would be hard-pressed to make enough money to support myself. Still, I felt like I had to do something – this belief being supported by the biblical teaching that 'if I don't work, I won't eat.' Being able to earn something was better than not earning anything.

I realized towards the end of my degree program that interpreting for the Deaf probably wouldn't be a good career match for me after all.

Still believing that I must be able to financially support myself, I dusted off my decades old resume and got to work. As I reviewed my skill set – and how long it's been since I actually used any of those skills – I came to the conclusion that they weren't worth enough for me to live on in the market at the time. That's when I opened my Etsy shop.

Even after a couple of years of working my shop, I still had no sustainable income and was still living off interest from my investments. I noticed that the principle balance had been pretty steady even though I'd been drawing from it every month for over 4 years. In my heart, I felt like Rod was still providing for me. So I began to wonder if I actually *needed* to find some other way to provide for myself financially. I took this question to prayer.

God revealed to me that I am provided for.

I will not be homeless; if the market crashes and I lose my home, I know people who will take me in. *I am provided for.*

I will not go hungry; there is a community food pantry where I can go to get food. Also I know people ...

I am provided for.

It may not look like it has before, but my physical needs will be met nonetheless. I began to believe it in my bones ...

I. Am. Provided. For.

Not like that baby bird I saw in my yard waiting, mouth agape, for provision to be brought to it, but like that bee. Everything I need has already been abundantly provided for me, and whatever I will need is already there, waiting to show up for me when I need it. All I have to do is see it.

Personal safety.

Rod was a brown belt in Taekwondo and a black belt with weapons training in Kenpo. And he loved me. Yeah, I felt pretty safe with him. So did I go out and get myself a black belt, or buff out my little 5'2" grandma self at the gym? Nope and nope.

I started looking at what I perceived to be dangers to my person, and asking if they actually were real threats to my safety. Most of them, I determined, were not.

For the ones that were actual potential dangers, I took

measures to prevent them. I have a home security system. I am selective as to where I go and when, and I pay attention to my surroundings when I'm out, and so on. I figure the best way to prevent danger is to avoid it.

But the biggest change in feeling safe took place in my mind. I realized that my thoughts were focused on all the bad things that could happen to me. I was looking for strangers around every corner who were going to jump out to steal my purse or hurt me. I expected every other driver on the road to swerve right in front of me and force me off a bridge or into a ditch somewhere. I watched sales people closely so they didn't steal from me. During the COVID pandemic, I was convinced that all people were germ-factories, and I was one interaction away from dying from covid.

The story I was telling myself was that people were dangerous to my safety and my well-being. Having these thoughts made me fearful of people, which caused me to be distrustful and suspicious, seeing every person as a potential threat in one way or another. In response, I kept my distance, which reinforced the thought that people were dangerous.

Does my life experience bear any evidence that people are out to get me? That answer is No. So what if I changed that thought? What if I chose to see people as neutral, just going about their own business, not paying attention to me at all? Would thinking that people are not my nemeses make a difference in how I feel and move through the world? I decided to conduct a little experiment.

Instead of avoiding people, I decided I would make eye contact, and maybe smile at them (making sure it was a real smile so it would show in my eyes if I was wearing a mask). I might even actually say words to perfect strangers!

I discovered people generally responded in kind. In one instance, after catching the eyes of someone clearly not having a good day, I smiled and commented that I liked their hair. Their whole demeanor changed! They smiled, thanked me, then proceeded to tell me the story about how their hair got that way.

Since I've been doing this – and I still do, even more so now – no one has jumped out from behind a corner to hurt me or try to steal from me. I acknowledge these concerns and do what I can to stay safe and to keep my body healthy, but I don't let fear make the final decisions. I don't know if I'm actually in less (or more) danger than I was before, but I've stopped fearing what *might* happen, and started enjoying what *is* happening.

As far as other drivers go, well, I just give them space to be ... themselves.

Companionship and Being Alone.

I had a built-in companion – a captive audience (sometimes to his chagrin), a ready shoulder, someone to go with me to the places I wanted to go. Someone to take care of and to take care of me. Someone to be my cheerleader, support me, share space with, to share life with. Rod was all these things to me.

Two months after Rod died, Kristyn went back to college for the spring semester. She came home on weekends and sometimes mid-week, but I was alone the rest of the time.

I had never lived alone, and I didn't know what to do with myself. I didn't know *how* to be alone.

I came across a poem on YouTube with that exact title, "How to Be Alone." I later found that this poem was actually in print, so I bought a copy (Tanya Davis, 2013). This poem brought concepts about being alone into my awareness that I never had before. There is a progression throughout the poem of getting to be ok with being alone, but the first few lines were all I could fathom at first. But it helped me to see that being alone didn't have to be a bad or a sad thing.

A big shift happened when I started learning that being alone was just spending time with myself. It started with small things, really.

Here's one: my idea of eating alone was that there was no one there to have a conversation with. I suppose I considered eating a social activity. I always felt bad when I saw someone eating alone, so of course I didn't like eating alone.

One morning I was eating a bowl of oatmeal alone and having myself a pity party about it. Well, that wasn't how I wanted to start my day, so I changed how I thought about eating alone. I thought about the food I was eating and everyone who was involved in getting the oats from the field into my bowl. That's a whole lotta people right there! I realized that I was talking out loud to myself by that time – *I was talking to myself!* I couldn't be alone if I had someone to talk to, now could I!

I changed the lens through which I looked at being alone. I shifted from looking through a lens of lack to one of abundance. I changed my self narrative from one of sadness to one of realizing that I am good company.

This shift was a big step towards learning how to be ok being alone, and being a companion to myself.

Validation/approval.

In April, 2016, I flew to California and drove back to Texas with my parents in their loaded-down car to move them into an assisted living place near me. My dad was pretty frail by that time, so he was unable to do much more than move himself – slowly – from one place to another. His wife had her own limitations, so much of the move was left up to me. Driving, lifting, handling phone calls and paperwork, shopping ...

I was with them at their new place, or tending to their business, every day for over a month helping them get settled in. Then I spent the next six months dealing with creditors and sorting through everything in their storage unit – tossing, donating, or moving it (a car load at a time) to my own garage – while still going to their place to visit 4-5 times per week.

My dad felt terrible that he couldn't help, and checked in with me on multiple occasions to make sure I was ok doing all the work. I'd reassure him, and remind him that he took care of me as a kid so it was my turn to take care of him now. He was worth it.

Once they were settled in and much of their stuff had been dealt with, I actually slowed down enough to see all that I had actually done – it was a lot! I desperately wanted someone to notice. I wasn't 'allowed' to point it out to anyone, because it was definitely not cool for me to 'toot my own horn.' There were a few times I thought my dad would say something, but he didn't.

If Rod were here, he would have been cheering me on the whole time, telling me how amazing I was. That's when I realized I was waiting for an acknowledgement and validation that was not coming.

One day, my dad asked me again how I managed to get everything done. My first thought was the expected response – I did it because I love you, because it's my turn, etc. – but I said none of these. After a short pause to consider my answer, I said to him, "Because I'm amazing, that's how!"

There. I said it. If no one else is going to say it, I am.

And you know what? No humble police came to haul me off, no one shamed me or opposed my proclamation. My dad looked at me a little surprised, laughed, and then called me a Lulu (something he'd affectionately call me when I was little, and being a little ... over the top, shall I say?).

External validation was one of those things I didn't realize I needed until it wasn't there. This experience showed me that I have it within myself to approve of myself, to be able to tell myself, "Good job, Gail! Way to go!"

Self-worth.

Living in the social framework that I do, I spent most of my life making myself small, keeping quiet and not making waves so everyone else is comfortable, and being subordinate to a whole lotta folks. I was valuable so long as I stayed in my place and did what was expected of me.

I remember a widow reminding me how much Rod valued and loved me. Wasn't that proof enough that I have worth and am lovable? Her comment gave me permission I didn't know I needed to value myself because of *who I am* rather than because of my gender or role – or any other external factor for that matter. It gave me the courage to step into that intrinsic value, and to realize and live into my inherent worth.

I started by paying attention to my face. Yes, my face. I didn't realize how frequently the muscles of my face were tense – my eyebrows, my lips, my jaw – making my whole face look angry or stressed or something else – it wasn't pleasant or approachable.

I'd heard somewhere that smiling could actually change how you feel, so whenever I realized my face was tense (and possibly expressing something I was not necessarily feeling), I relaxed those muscles, and then I smiled. That actually did make a difference right in the moment.

For example, if I realize that my face is tense while I'm washing dishes or doing laundry and I choose to smile, the task suddenly seems more enjoyable. Or if I find myself in a tense situation, smiling actually alleviates the tension not only in my face but also in my body, allowing me to think more clearly and not react emotionally.

I've noticed that smiling can also diffuse the tension of a situation. I was once faced with a potential conflict with a difficult person in my life, and I checked my face. I'm not sure, but I'm pretty sure I looked like I was ready for a fight (even though that was the last thing I wanted!). I consciously relaxed my face and chose to smile, and the situation became a lot less confrontational. I avoided the conflict by simply smiling.

I'd also heard about the mind-body connection; your body

can also inform your emotions and how you feel. So I decided to test this out, too.

When I adjust my posture to stand straight – dropping my shoulders (I didn't realize how often they were creeping up towards my ears!) and lifting my chin – I feel more confident. When I walk with longer strides and with purpose rather than taking small unsteady steps like I'm perpetually in someone's way, I find that people make space for me. And when I set my eyes to look straight ahead meeting the eyes of people I pass, I feel like I belong. I found that making adjustments in my body *did* affect my emotions and how I feel and, consequently, how I move through and interact with the world.

It felt weird at first, like I was trying to be someone I was not. Imposter syndrome. But when I did these things I found there was space for me in the world, and I deserved to be in it. I wasn't pretending; I was behaving like the person I wanted to become – a confident, complete individual occupying my own space and knowing that I belong. Like I used to feel walking beside Rod.

Each of these interactions and experiences has been an opportunity for me to learn to meet my own needs, and to take care of myself – things Rod had always done for me. **The more I am able to take care of myself – to meet my own needs – the more confidence I gain, and the more complete a person I become.**

Learning to meet my own needs, which is in essence learning to love myself, has changed my perspective on marriage, and on love itself.

I needed Rod to complete me. Is this need actually love?

Can need and love become so intermingled that they become synonymous, indistinguishable from one another? They did for me, love being based on whether or not it could meet my needs.

Because my relationship of 30+ years was based on this need-based love, I don't know what a marriage relationship *not* based on need would look like. I don't know what it would look like to be partners without needing to meet each other's needs.

The question I wrestle with is this: If I have within myself the capacity to meet all my own needs, and if marriage is based on need, then what would be the point of being married? Without the need to complete one another, why marry?

I don't have an answer to that. I mean, if I can dance around in my kitchen by myself and enjoy that just as much as dancing around in my kitchen with someone else, then why would I need them? Perhaps it's just to have somebody to share that moment with, or for the simple satisfaction of being seen. Or maybe it's just about dancing together.

What does love look like if I am my own person and I don't need someone else to complete me? I am still sorting through the idea that the only reason to have a partner is to meet each other's needs.

My relationship with God before Rod died reflected this idea of need-based love. I was taught that God loves me unconditionally; I am his creation, and nothing can ever take that away from me. Be that as it may, when it comes to me loving God, if I was honest with myself, would I love God if I didn't need him for my personal salvation? What would loving God look like if I didn't need him to save me?

But my need for Him extends beyond my eternal salvation, I was told. I was taught that I *absolutely* needed God — every day in every way and to meet every need I could ever have. I am so "desperately wicked" that I cannot live without God; I *need* Him for my very existence.

What might a relationship with God look like if I came to Him as a complete, whole person? I don't mean having everything together or being sinless, but acknowledging the truth of who I *could* be, and being open to experiencing all that He created me to be. What if I could simply exist with God, just being present? Perhaps love is presence.

TWO

Faith

"When we experience tragedy, heartache,
or disappointment,
What happens right now in our spirit -
What happens to us emotionally,
what happens to us spiritually -
Will be more impactful than the actual event itself.

How we respond ...will be much more impactful for us
than the actual event.

So, the question is ...

How are we going to respond?"

Rod Bayron, "The Art of Bouncing Back"

II

Religious Background

I grew up in the Catholic faith, and went through catechism. I received my First Holy Communion by about age six. It was a big deal – I wore a white dress with a veil and white tights and new white patent leather shoes. All three of my living grandparents were there, and everyone was so proud of me. I have scattered memories from before this, and shortly thereafter, like fading photos in which I don't recognize the people or recall the particulars of practicing my faith with my family.

After my mom passed away when I was 12, my dad, brother, and I said lots of rosaries together. My dad tried to make church-going a regular thing for the three of us, but these efforts were short-lived.

About a year later, I made a new friend in school. She, like me, didn't seem to 'fit in' but, unlike me, she didn't seem

to mind. One day, I asked her why. She said she found acceptance in Jesus, and told me I could, too.

So I gave my life to Jesus in a profession of faith to Him,
and I told my dad about my decision. He was desperately
missing connection in his life, so he also decided to follow
Jesus, too.

He and I started attending the church where my friend
went with her family. The people there didn't behave like they
did in the Catholic church. There were no kneelers, no holy
water, and no one stopped to genuflect before taking their
seat in the pew.

It was a large church with a thriving youth group that I
was more than happy to jump into with my friend. I learned
about Jesus while sitting on a comfy couch surrounded by
posters and string lights on the walls. We looked for opportunities to live in a way that Jesus would approve of as we
attended youth rallies, lock-ins, and summer camps. I learned
what it was like to be part of a Christian community and
what it meant to have a church family with lots of 'spiritual'
siblings!

The God I met there was not like the God I experienced
in the Catholic church as a young girl.

That God of my childhood was distant, reached only
through the piety and spirituality of the priests, a God who
demanded penance for every misstep and weekly restoration
through communion.

But the God I met as a teen at my friend's church was
accessible and amenable; He was our friend. He was someone
to be personally experienced, not adored from afar through
ritual and in somberness. He was involved directly in the

lives of parishoners – Scriptures could be read privately in our own Bibles, sins could be confessed directly to Him without the need for a priest in a confessional, and joy could be imbued upon us directly by God himself. This God understood the sinful, rebellious nature of these human creatures He created and their propensity to wander, but He was patient and waited with open, loving arms for the wayward child (or youth) to return to Him.

Of course, there was still a penalty for sin. This God was no less just than the God I met in my early religious training, but He was more about grace and everything was couched in love.

Granted, it had been some years since I'd attended a Catholic church, and my memories reflected the experience of a young child, but it was the only experience I had, my only point of reference to church, or to God. I liked this new understanding of God much better. He accepted me as and where I was.

It wasn't long before my friend moved away, and Dad and I found a smaller church, more to his liking. The teaching was solid and the music more ... traditional. Understanding the importance of being part of a community, I made friends with the few other teens that attended this church, but it wasn't the same.

My dad remarried when I was 16. We moved to a different city to be closer to his new wife's job. The three of us started attending a mega-church nearby, and I got involved in the very large, very active youth group.

Rod had also grown up Catholic, and also accepted Christ as a teen by reading a tract that had been left in the men's room at the beach, but he wasn't attending church at that time, and my church attendance was limited to Saturday night concerts and youth events.

Once I outgrew the youth scene, I stopped going to church.

Rod and I got engaged on our high school graduation day, got married at 20, and moved halfway across the country for his job when we were 23, with our first child being just over one year old. Nine months after our big move, our second son was born.

We were supposed to be on assignment with this job in Texas for 18 months to three years before returning home, so I hadn't put much effort into making friends. After about two years it started to look like we might be here to stay; I began to feel the loss of family and community as I lost hope of returning home.

Every week on my way to and from the grocery store, I passed by a little church on the corner, behind a 7-Eleven. When I realized that we were going to be in Texas for the long haul, and that I desperately needed friends, I wondered if that little church might be a good place to find them. Week after week, the pull to check out this church grew stronger, so one Sunday Rod and I got ourselves and the boys up and dressed, and we went to that little church called Audelia Road Baptist Church (ARBC).

It was different being in a Protestant church as an adult than as a youth. There were kids seated or running about the sanctuary, and adults clumped together talking in small and large groups all around the church – before and after the service. Just about everyone had their own Bible, but there were extra copies in the built-in racks on the backs of the pews for anyone who didn't. People read along with the pastor, and some even wrote in their Holy Bibles! (We were barely allowed to touch our family Catholic bible, much less *write* in it!)

And church didn't only happen on Sundays ...

We had monthly potluck dinners at our mid-week prayer services, Tuesday morning ladies' Bible studies, and exercise groups three days a week. There were Sunday School parties, group mission trips, and even a church-wide family camp one year. These were the times that served the church body. They were events that forged and shaped relationships between individuals and whole families within this body of believers. This was where life happened for us – in God's house among God's people, sharing food, sharing needs, sharing life.

These were folks Rod and I served with in both Christian and humanitarian efforts. **These were friends who became family; this was my community and my support system as I navigated life with all its ups and down, its twists and turns.**

In the 12 years Rod and I attended and served together at ARBC, we grew and became grounded in our Christian faith. This is where I learned – by instruction and by example – what it meant to be a Godly wife and a virtuous woman. Having been raised in the 60s with the mindset of "a woman's place" being in the home, I was already there; adding Biblical support and spiritual rewards for obedience to God and husband only strengthened my resolve and deepened my conviction in the proper way for me to fulfill my role and responsibilities.

Rod and I were baptized there, as were all of our kids. Rod and I became firm in our Baptist beliefs and confident in our eternal destiny. Many of my faith-related questions were answered there; I knew what I knew, and I was satisfied that I had found the truth. I found so much more than friends there. It was a good – and safe – place for us and our young family to grow up.

Circumstances drew us away from this little church on the corner that had protected and grown us and our family in our faith and so much more. A number of years after leaving ARBC, we landed at Clearwater Community Church (C3) and we settled in. But this time we were coming in from a place of experience and knowledge; Rod and I both found ourselves in leadership roles before too long.

We made friends here, too, other couples we'd serve with and share a different stage of life with. Instead of swapping baby-sitting and hand-me-down clothes, we were staring into the quickly approaching empty nest and learning how to care for aging parents.

Our beliefs remained strong, and the Bible continued to be our guiding star in how to live life. We had experienced God – corporately, as a couple, and individually – in different ways and many situations, and God generally showed up according to our expectations based on our understanding of the Bible. On those occasions that He didn't respond as anticipated, we chalked it up to His perfect wisdom and/or timing, made adjustments, and went on.

I still had questions here and there, but for each one I was given an answer. Most of them made sense and satisfied my musings. For those that didn't, I acknowledged the supremacy and mystery of God's wisdom, and that was good enough for me.

It was during our time at C3 when Rod's cancer was diagnosed, and when he passed.

12

Evolving Spirituality

About a month after Rod's diagnosis, I read an entry from a devotional book that had been given to us while Rod was in the hospital. The verse for that day hit me square between the eyes. It was Job 5:18, which says, "For he wounds, but he binds up; he shatters, but his hands heal."

Did I just read a promise from God that He will heal Rod's cancer?!? I shared the verse with Rod.

He read the verse himself, looked at me with wide eyes, read the verse again, and told me that maybe I did.

I already believed that God *could* heal Rod's cancer, but I believed this was a promise from God directly to me that He *would* heal Rod.

Through all of Rod's treatments, our friends were there for us, one hundred percent. They diligently prayed for us – healing for his body, strength for our faith, encouragement for our spirits. They'd check in and offer whatever help would be useful.

We were doing all the right things, exactly as we were instructed in the Bible. Casting all our cares on Him. Praying without ceasing. Trusting that God had it handled. Praying believing – the mountain-moving kind of belief. Praying without wavering that whatever we ask in Jesus' name will be given. And I gave thanks whenever I could find something to be grateful for, and searched for anything when I couldn't.

We continued going to church every Sunday that Rod was physically able to go. We kept his doctor's appointments, doing everything they said to do, trusting these doctors because we believed they were participating in the healing that God was going to bring. We even continued to plan for our upcoming mission trip to Israel, including getting the doctor's approval for Rod to travel. What could show more faith than planning a trip in spite of the cancer?

We did our part, and waited anxiously for God to do His – to move that mountain that was Rod's cancer. I was convinced that we'd one day be on the 'other side' of this trial, giving God all the glory for miraculously healing this horrendous disease. There would be lifestyle adjustments afterwards, of course, but I *knew* there would be an afterwards.

I believed this so completely that I would not tolerate any discussion of the possibility of Rod dying from this. I believed that to talk about Rod dying would be a chink in my faith armor. It would be showing doubt, being "like a wave of the sea driven and tossed by the wind" (James 1:6) which would have a direct impact on the outcome of my prayers. No, no, this wouldn't do. I was praying for the impossible here, for his cancer to be healed, so why would I plan for an outcome that wasn't going to happen?

I think Rod tried to talk to me about it a number of times, but I wouldn't participate in a discussion of that sort, believing God was going to heal him. We needed to focus on him getting better, not planning his funeral!

There were a number of times he would bypass the discussion and just blurt out what he wanted – what his service should be like, who he wanted to speak and who to lead the worship songs, blah, blah, blah. (I did actually pay attention and even wrote down and honored the things he said he wanted.)

We had one very short discussion years ago when I was trying to pre-plan for us both that went like this:

Me: Do you want to be buried or cremated when you die?
Rod: Cremated.
Me: What do you want me to do with your ashes?
Rod: What do I care? I'm dead.

That was as far as our pre-planning ever went.

One of the things he blurted out just months before he died came while we were driving, approaching the huge cemetery near our city. He casually said, "I think I'd like to be buried" just like that, out of the blue – well, at least to my thinking.

"I thought you wanted to be cremated," I responded. Then I asked where he wanted to be buried. He pointed to the cemetery as we were passing by and said, "There." That was it.

In retrospect, I wonder if he remembered our earlier

discussion (which was had more than once), and decided being buried in a cemetery might be better for me. But we didn't talk about the kids, the house, or what my future might look like without him. None of it. I didn't think we needed to. We were doing everything just as it was laid out for us in the Bible, and God was going to heal him.

In spite of our spiritual diligence, Rod was not getting better. Things were not even progressing according to how his oncologist indicated they would.

The oncologist's plan from the get-go was to hit the tumor hard with six weeks of radiation treatments five times per week along with a drip pack (that we named John) that dripped chemo directly into the port they'd inserted in his chest the day he left the hospital back in April. He wore his iDrip (as we referred to it, trying to inject irony and humor into a surreal situation) like a cross-body bag. Being attached to his body, John was a constant companion for those six weeks, making its presence known at our daughter-in-law Glennda's college graduation and the birth of our second grandchild.

Once the radiation was done and John's task was complete, we had to wait a number of weeks to do another scan to see how much the tumor had shrunk. The tumor was on the head of Rod's pancreas, right near the little hook shape that went around two main arteries that run right through the digestive system. We didn't need the tumor to go completely away with these initial treatments; all the surgeon needed was a tiny margin between the tumor and these arteries to perform a pancreaticoduodenectomy, also known as the Whipple procedure. This is a pretty invasive surgery that would take some time to recover from, and it would require major dietary and lifestyle changes afterwards, but it would save his life.

In the meantime, we'd make weekly visits to the oncology office where I'd spend two to three hours sitting next to Rod and watching (and fighting back tears) as they'd drip huge bags of poison directly into his chest.

The time finally came for the test, and then we had to wait some more for the results. While sitting on pins and needles, we continued to pray without ceasing. I envisioned looking at that image provided by the lab and seeing the tumor not only smaller but actually gone, sparing Rod the need for surgery and the difficult road that would surely follow. I believed with my whole being, not wavering, not doubting; I just *knew* that the imaging test would yield the results we were looking for.

But it didn't. The tumor seemed to measure almost the exact same size as when we started. The doctor was actually pleased; he said pancreatic tumors are aggressive, and the fact that it stopped growing was a big deal!

He told us the image was inconclusive. It was possible that the tumor itself had shrunk and that what the image was picking up was scar tissue from the radiation treatments.

So they sent a copy of the image to the surgical oncologist, and we went in for a consultation with him. He agreed that the image was unclear; however, it showed enough for him to conclude that the margins they'd hoped for were not there. We talked about continued treatments, and I asked about lifestyle or diet changes we could make to help this process along. He gave us some suggestions, but followed it all up with "But if you want pizza, eat pizza." As far as physical activity, he said whatever Rod wanted to do and felt strong enough to do he should do.

On the drive back to work, we talked about his suggestions, and suddenly it hit me – *did he just give us the end-of-life/quality-of-life speech? Is that what that just was?!?*

No, no, no. Couldn't be. He was *supposed* to say there was just enough room to operate. He was *supposed* to say it would be operable after the next round of treatments. He was *supposed* to say keep on avoiding cancer-feeding foods and recommend cancer-fighting exercises. His assessment had to be premature.

God was going to heal Rod's body. I couldn't understand why he hadn't started healing it already. Why had he allowed it to continue to get worse?

When we got back to work after the appointment. Rod parked and started to get out of the car to head back into the office. I didn't move. He sat back down and waited; he could see that I needed a minute.

I could not figure out why God wasn't making the tumor shrink or go away. Did I not have enough faith? Was I doing something wrong, something that was blocking my prayers?

This couldn't be right. God wouldn't leave us hanging like this. He just wouldn't.

It took a few minutes for me to compose myself enough to go back into the office. I noted the absurdity of Rod being the one to console and encourage me when it was in his body that this life-sucking monster resided.

Treatments continued in weeks-long rounds with more tests in between chemo cocktails, all showing little to no change in the size of the tumor, meaning little to no chance of surgery. And Rod continued to lose weight and strength.

Getting similar results from subsequent tests sent me into fits of tears every time. But I couldn't break down in front of Rod – I had to be strong for him. Rod was no longer a safe place for me to feel everything I was trying desperately not to show him. I had to find time and space to fall apart by myself, grieving the loss of him being my safe place along with everything else.

Something happened a few weeks before he died that made me think he had been doing the same thing – being strong for me.

I went to check on him (he spent a lot of time in bed by that point) after composing myself after a good quiet cry, alone. To my surprise, I could see that he, too, had been crying. We held each other and sobbed together. I didn't realize until that moment that he had actually been my safe place this whole time. We did need to be strong to walk through this trial, but seeing each other's grief gave us permission to grieve together.

For every report that showed there was no change or improvement, I believed beyond the test. Every time a new problem was discovered, I saw it as one more victory we'd claim later after God had healed it all.

When Rod coded on the cancer floor in the hospital the night he died, Kristyn and I stood out in the hallway, sobbing through loudly vocalized pleading prayers to God, acknowledging how absolutely miraculous it would be for God to step in at this critical moment and heal his body. *There would be no way anyone could take credit for this one, God. Everyone would know it was all you! Way to maximize and glorify your name!*

Even after he died, I found myself thinking it still wasn't too late. I remembered the story of the widow's son in Luke 7, of Jairus' daughter from Mark 5, and of Jesus calling Lazarus from his tomb in John 11. I even recalled the story of how God brought a whole army to life by reanimating dry, sun-bleached bones, literally breathing life back into them with the four winds in Ezekiel 37.

And I continued to hope for a miracle.

We'd done everything we knew to do, just like we'd been doing for the past seven months. It was God's turn now, and he was nowhere to be found.

Rod was still dead.

In the months following his death, my faith remained strong. I chose to believe that it was Rod's appointed time to die, that God was still God and still on His throne, and He was still going to take care of me.

But as the widow fog began to clear, I found it was increasingly difficult for me to reconcile my lived experience with my understanding and expectation of God. I began to feel deep betrayal and anger towards Him.

I had an experience with Kristyn, my daughter, that beautifully illustrates my feelings towards God at this point.

When she was two or three years old, Rod and I went to a weekend marriage retreat. Our best friends (and our kids' god-parents) and their toddler stayed at the house for the weekend to take care of our three kids, the pets and the house.

When we arrived home, Kristyn came running to me, arms up in the familiar 'pick me up' posture, so I did. She was very squirmy; not wanting to drop her, I put her back down on the floor. She immediately let out a cry of discontent and leaned heavily on my legs, her arms once again extended upwards, so I picked her up again. She started squirming around in my arms again, but I realized this time that she was trying to turn around so that she was facing away from me; I helped her complete her goal, but she was still unhappy and continued to squirm. I put her down again, which she immediately – vocally and physically – objected to.

Not knowing what she wanted, I moved to the couch and she followed practically under my feet. As soon as I sat down, up went her little arms once more, so I picked her up and sat her on my lap facing me; I tried to hold her close, but she would have none of it. No longer fearful of dropping her on the ground, I let her try to figure herself out.

She turned herself around on my lap with her back towards me, and she scooted herself to the edge of my knees getting as far from my body as she could. I placed my hands around her torso to steady her, but she pushed them off not wanting me to touch her, while maintaining her balance as best she could on my knees. Every time I started to put her down so I could stand up, she lost it. She threw herself into my legs, arms reaching up.

She was so very angry with me for leaving, but she was also going to make darn sure I didn't leave her again!

Like Kristyn told me through her actions, I told God, *I don't want anything to do with you, God. Don't touch me. But don't you dare let me go!*

I knew how this was supposed to go. I kept up my end of the bargain, but when it was His turn, He bailed. How can He expect me to obey Him when it doesn't matter whether or not I did in the end? I understand that everyone dies, but how could he keep misleading us – me – with all His talk about throwing mountains into the sea, feeding 5,000 people with a little boy's lunch, and raising people from the dead? *Where was all that power, God? Clearly you were capable of healing Rod at any point; you simply chose not to. You chose to let him die. And you broke the promise you made specifically to me.*

I honestly think I'd have felt differently if I thought He didn't have the power to do it. I'd at least be able to say, *You gave it your best shot, God. Thanks for trying.* But I *know* He could have healed him, if He wanted to.

So I can only conclude that He didn't want to, that He wanted Rod to die. Which, by extension, means that He *wanted* me to be widowed at 51. He *wanted* our grandbabies to never know their Lolo. And He *wanted* me to drift aimlessly through life, bereft of role and purpose in this world, and for me to grow old alone. And I'm young enough to potentially have a good number of years to live out this sentence.

No, this was not the God I had learned about in church. *That* God was my friend. *That* God wanted the best for me. *That* God was full of love and grace. That was not the God I was experiencing in the aftermath.

I was faced with a conundrum: what I understood to be true about God did not line up with my lived experience of Him. One of these things was in error, and – despite my feelings – I was still pretty sure it wasn't God. So I began to ask the question, *God, if you are not who I've always thought you*

were – who I've always believed you to be – then who are you?
And so began my search for God.

I suppose this could be considered a prayer, so I could say
the first place I searched for God was in prayer. But it didn't
feel like any prayer I'd ever prayed before, or heard prayed in
church or any prayer meeting I'd ever been to. It didn't follow
the ACTS (Adoration, Confession, Thanksgiving, Supplica-
tion) format, it didn't apply the Five Finger method of who
to pray for, or even follow the example of the Lord's Prayer
in Matthew 5. No, I couldn't pray those kinds of prayers. In
fact, I couldn't really pray at all – unless I could call having a
tantrum at God a prayer.

Prayer, as I had understood and experienced it prior to
this, was near impossible for me at this point. Not only was I
unable to pray on my own, but I realized that I was checking
out when I heard other people pray. What was the point?

If God knows the end from the beginning, and His will
will always be accomplished, then why should I waste my
time asking for something that He has already willed to
happen – or not happen – and for which He already knows
the outcome? How can he tell me to pray for a mountain to
move when He has already decided it's going to stay right
where it is?

It would be like telling my kids that they could ask me
for anything they want; let's say they want to go to Disneyland. I tell them to clean their rooms, eat all their veggies, do
all their chores and their homework, and get good grades in
school. Not just today, but continually. They can ask me to
go to Disneyland as often as they want to while they're doing

everything I told them to do. And if I don't answer, that just means Wait …

All the while, I know I have no intention of taking them to Disneyland. But I don't tell them this. I just let them hope in vain knowing that no matter how well (or poorly) they adhere to my conditions the answer will be No. But, hey, it's sure nice not stepping on Legos or throwing away perfectly good food.

Once the kids figured this out, they'd want to know why I made them do all those things. I would tell them it was for their own good – to build good habits so they could become better people. Unfortunately, it's likely that all those good habits will go by the wayside because, for the kids, they were merely a means to an end. An end that didn't come, an end that was never going to come.

Somewhere in my church experience, I learned that prayer is for our benefit, to help us shift our focus from our problem to God's power and blah, blah, blah. (Yeah, that was one of those teachings I found myself rolling my eyes at.)

But it did not build good habits in me, and all that prayer didn't make me a better person. Or save Rod. The only thing I could see that prayer helped me shift was my view of God from being loving and benevolent to being distant, disinterested and uncaring.

Prayers were a means to an end; in all practicality they were outcome-based. We were told that God is not a "vending machine" where we deposit our prayers and good works in order to get our desired outcome, but taking prayer requests in Sunday School sure looked exactly like that.

All during Rod's illness, I was praying how I knew to pray.

I spent seven months in constant fervent prayer and it didn't amount to squat. So I went through a long period after his death where I just didn't see a point to it.

I have not gone back to this outcome-based model of prayer. In fact, I make it a point not to ask God for anything. Ever.

So if the outcome of my prayers is not the point, then what is?

I had an experience that put me on a path to an answer to this question, redefining what prayer is for me.

I was standing on the earth, thinking about how the earth supports me. I wondered at the largeness of our planet, and how a spherical object can seem flat from my vantage point. I trusted the earth to support me, that I could walk on it, run on it, lay on it, jump on it all without worry or concern that I would fall off it; it would always be there to catch me.

I thought about the electrical impulses that run through the earth that positively affect my body and bring it back to health and into balance. I asked nothing more of the earth than it was already offering; I simply accepted it.

Maybe that's what prayer is – simply acknowledging and being in God's presence, wondering at His greatness. Trusting without worry or concern that He is supporting me, always there to catch me. Observing the positive effect He has on my being. And asking nothing more of Him than He has already abundantly provided, and simply accepting it. Maybe prayer is simply being present with God.

Another place I searched for God was in my Bible.

As I read Scripture, I found myself thinking, *Oh, I know*

this verse. I've read it (probably more than once) and likely heard a sermon or two about it, and this is what it means. Hearing this narrative in my head made me realize that I had God all tied up in a neat little box with a bow. *This verse means that. For everyone. For always. Amen.* There was a single "right" answer or understanding of Scripture, and I knew what that answer was.

Until I didn't.

The first time I read a verse differently was just months after Rod died. In Luke 24:39, Jesus said, "Look at my hands and my feet. It is I myself! Touch me and see; a ghost does not have flesh and bones, as you see I have."

record scratch

Come again, Jesus? A **what** doesn't have flesh and bones?

Sure, the disciples were afraid because they thought they were seeing a ghost, but if ghosts didn't exist – and apparently able to be seen by the living – why would Jesus have said anything about them at all?

So Jesus basically said ghosts are a thing. Well, at least in the New International Version translation. Other translations use the word spirit. Either way that means that Rod could possibly be a spirit somewhere near me! Clearly he wouldn't have flesh and bones and I wouldn't be able to touch him, as Jesus so clearly pointed out, but I'd apparently be able to see him.

I'd always believed that to be absent from the body was to be present with the Lord, that once we die we are immediately taken up into God's presence and have no more need or desire to be concerned with the affairs of this earth. This verse directly challenged that belief, seeming to suggest the possibility that Rod's spirit could possibly still be around. I didn't expect that I'd be able to see his spirit like the disciples thought they saw Jesus' spirit, but maybe I could feel his presence.

I began to wonder what nuggets might be hidden in other verses, those certain parts of them that were typically skipped over in sermons, or just generally not taught or even talked about.

So I started reading the Bible differently. I tried to read each verse as though for the first time, not forgetting what I had been taught about it but being open to the possibility that there might be a different interpretation or understanding of these familiar verses. I was earnestly seeking God Himself, and He promised I'd find Him, whatever that was worth. But, promise notwithstanding, I continued to search.

I read a book called What Is The Bible by Rob Bell (HarperCollins, 2017), which helped me in this endeavor. In his introduction, he says,

"But the bible is a book about what it means to be human. ... This is a book about a library of books dealing with loss and anger and transcendence and worry and empire and money and fear and stress and joy and doubt and grace and healing ..."

Jesus used parables to talk about this humanness that we all share. Did the father and sons in the story of the prodigal son exist in reality? Was the good samaritan a real person? Here's the thing. It doesn't really matter if they were real or made up; the stories were about being human with all the messy emotions and consequences that come with being human. They are relatable to anyone. We are the ones longing for a loved one to return, or the ones who have come face-to-face with the consequences of our own bad choices. And we are the ones who pass by people every day who have been beaten down by life, or maybe we're the one who has been beaten down, waiting for someone to reach out a hand.

These characters are us in real life situations; the specifics of these parables were created by Jesus for the purpose of teaching us a life lesson. They can reach anyone – the father or the son, the Pharisee, the Samaritan or the traveler.

Jesus taught in parables because they were relatable; they are relevant to us – no matter where in the story we see ourselves – and can have a direct impact on our personal lives.

It would make sense, then, for the rest of the bible to also have parables rather than to be completely historical or literal.

Literal stories are interesting, but there is a distance between them and us. They are accounts of long ago events and dead people – not relevant to my life right here and right now. I don't see myself in the historical events of Daniel or Jonah, for example.

But, if I read the story of Daniel as a parable instead of a historical event, that's when it gets real. Rob Bell shares how Daniel's is a story about a person "who's stripped of his name and family and customs ... Everything known and familiar is taken from him ..." (p. 304)

This I understand – my life without Rod, without Rod's Wife, without that life that was comfortable and safe and familiar. But through it all, "... [Daniel] maintains his sense of self ..." (p. 304) This gives me hope that a sense of self might exist for me in the aftermath of my loss. It won't look like Daniel's experience, but the loss and the hope are real.

And if I read Jonah as something other than one guy's weird personal experience long ago in a foreign land, I see a person who is angry at God – angry enough to go to great lengths to avoid what inevitably lies ahead, but still ends up having to do the thing. And then still be angry about it after the fact. Can I connect with this? You betcha! I was angry at God and tried desperately to avoid what eventually came to pass – I am still a widow, despite all my attempts to ignore, deny, and run from it. This reality swallowed me whole and spat me out unrecognizable. And I've had plenty of moments where I sat under my own fig tree just mad about not being Rod's wife anymore.

I stopped reading my bible like it was a history book or an instruction manual. I started reading the stories like they were parables, relevant to my own life – right here, right now.

Then (by divine coincidence?) I discovered a contemplative way to read the bible through a 16th century Spanish Catholic priest, Ignatius of Loyola. His method uses visualization as a way to put yourself in the story for the purpose of encountering Jesus. This sounded interesting, so I looked up his spiritual exercises, and gave it a try.

It's very involved and it takes quite a time commitment to follow the method completely, but just following a few of the principles as I read through the gospels, imagining that I was there beside Jesus – whether as an observer or as someone interacting with him – brought the whole parable thing to a new level.

I imagined myself at the wedding in Cana where Jesus

changed water to wine (John 2). As a wedding guest, what smells might I have smelled? What would I have been wearing, and how far would I have walked to get there – would I have been tired? Dusty? Would I have been aware of the miracle that was about to transpire?

What might it have been like if I were one of the servants following Mary's orders to do whatever Jesus said? Did I just fill the containers with water, drop them off and leave? Or perhaps I stayed and watched the water begin to change color – what might I have felt witnessing that? How heavy were those barrels, and were there other servants there helping me carry them from the well to the wedding site?

I imagined what it might have been like for John the Baptist the day Jesus walked by the river where he was doing his thing in John 1. What might he have felt when at least two of his disciples rushed to follow Jesus once he pointed the Messiah out to them? Did anyone else follow Andrew and the other of John's disciples?

What might Andrew have felt, following Jesus – did he have a "fangirl" moment after learning so much about Jesus from John? And, later, how might he have approached his brother, Simon (v.40-42) – full of excitement? Out of breath and talking fast?

This made such a difference for me! The people in these stories represented the human experience with its real – and sometimes messy – human emotions. I was learning to approach the bible in a way other than intellectually, or even habitually. I allowed the stories to play out in my mind like a movie where I paid attention to all the things surrounding the main story – the sets and props, side characters, the background sounds, the scents in the air …

Reading my bible became a whole different experience for me. I started to see beyond history and interpretation, and to experience a different layer of understanding of an event or a conversation. It made the bible so much more interesting, and relevant to where I am in my life and to who I am becoming.

And I was seeing God in a different light than I had ever seen Him before. My conundrum was beginning to fade – I wasn't seeing opposing versions of God. He is not either this or that; He is both/and. Once again, I found that my previous knowledge and experience – this time about what I believed to be true of God – was not incorrect, it was incomplete.

I got curious about God's presence in nature, in the cosmos, and even in people, searching for His fingerprint in this world that He created. Art is an expression of the artist who created it; they imbue something of themselves into everything they create. It would stand to reason (at least to me), then, that I can learn something about God if I observe and study His creation.

I'm not talking about studying the different species of birds, or knowing the names of all the trees in my neighborhood. Or even what life lessons I might learn from nature. I'm talking about what that something of God might be that has been imbued within each of His creations.

What different aspects of God might I see as I observe His creation? What might these observations reveal about Him?

As I mentioned earlier, I noticed how the earth supports me, catches me when I fall, and recharges my battery, in a manner of speaking. What I was doing as I connected with that part of God that was imbued into the earth was connecting to God himself. In this way, I could experience God's steadfastness, His abundant provision for nurturing, growth, and healing.

I once saw a mama Robin catch a wasp, beat it on a brick until the stinger came off, then feed it to its baby. In this, I witness the fierceness with which God provides for those in need.

I can count on the sun coming up every morning, making its course through the sky, and setting every evening. It offers its benefits to the earth and everything that lives on it. In this, I understand God's constant and predictable presence that nurtures all of creation.

What aspects of himself might God have imbued within a bee, or in the flowers they pollinate? Or in the mountains, or in the moon or the stars?

I searched for Him in the monotony of the mundane, in other belief systems, and even within myself. The Bible says He's everywhere, so I looked everywhere. And I'm still finding Him in so many ways and places I'd never thought to look before.

In all of my searching for God, I am learning that nothing exists in a bubble. Everything and everyone is interconnected; we are all works of the same Artist.

I am finding God to be an ineffable mystery. He is so much bigger and more mysterious than I ever could have imagined.

The more He reveals Himself to me, the greater the mystery He becomes. And I am learning to sit in that unknowing, and to see beyond the duality of this world.

I am sitting with the idea that God is love, quite literally, as John says in chapter 4 of 1 John. God is not the embodiment of love, not the perfect example of it, or even the definition of it. Love is not a feeling or a verb; it is not something to possess, and it is not an aspect of God. God is Love itself.

> *Love is patient, love is kind. It does not envy, it does not boast, it is not proud. It does not dishonor others, it is not self-seeking, it is not easily angered, it keeps no record of wrongs. Love does not delight in evil but rejoices with the truth. It always protects, always trusts, always hopes, always perseveres. Love never fails. (I Cor 13:5-8a NIV)*

The God I am discovering is all of these things *because* *He is Love.*

> *God is love. When we take up permanent residence in a life of love, we live in God and God lives in us. (I John 4:17, MSG)*

When we have love, we have God. Because God *is* love. These discoveries have all but undone everything I have believed about Jehova God; they have brought me such an expansive understanding of the existence of the Divine than I have ever known. God as I knew Him in my religion hasn't been replaced, just expanded. The Divine I am discovering is so much more than the God I knew.

13

Church Without Rod

Rod and I rarely missed a Sunday morning service at church. I figured if Rod were still here, we'd still be going, so I continued going to church faithfully after he died. It may have been out of habit at first as I tried desperately to maintain some modicum of normalcy, but more importantly it was comfortable and familiar. It was the place where I was loved, accepted, and cared for. It was where my friends were. So I continued going. Even as a widow.

When Rod first died, Kristyn and her oldest brother and his family were still attending C3. Early the next year, the church relocated, but there were about three or four months between the time the old lease ran out and the new building was ready, so we were meeting in the classrooms of another church. My oldest and his family were there during this interim, but Kristyn stopped coming. When we moved into our new facility, she joined us once again.

It was kinda sorta like it used to be; we took up a whole row like we used to, and everybody knew that was the Bayron row – just like that was the Davies' row, and that one was the Walker's row. I mean, we all kind of sat in the same general area every Sunday, so we all knew who sat where. (That made leaving random Secret Sister gifts pretty easy!)

But it was different. Rod was in on the planning of this new facility, but he never got to find his place here. He was not only absent from our row, he never had a presence in it. There were no memories of Rod in this place – no holiday plays, no classrooms where he taught bible study. He never got to play his guitar with the worship team in this place.

In the fall of 2014, our oldest son and his family moved about three and a half hours south of where I live, and then it was just me and Kristyn.

It wasn't long before Kristyn stopped coming. Then it was just me.

I sat in the Bayron family row, alone. The vacancies that surrounded me were deafening. So I started sitting in different places but always keeping an eye on 'our' row, noting if it remained vacant or if others sat there.

I remember some days getting to church and walking in through the back doors of the worship center and pausing there for a minute to see where I might sit. And there were more than a few Sundays that I turned around and went right back home because I didn't see any other option other than to sit by myself.

I remember one Sunday sitting with no one in particular, surrounded by people I knew. As we stood up to sing a song, a friend sitting in front of me reached her arm through her husband's and pulled in close. I left before the song was over. I remembered how many times I'd done the same thing with Rod, and I suddenly felt very alone. His absence was all I could see, and I just couldn't do it.

There was another Sunday morning service, as the communion trays were being passed through the congregation, I watched my friend's husband take the tray. He took one cup out and handed it to her, took one out for himself, and then passed the tray in front of her to give it to the next person. It was just a little way that he took care of her. Rod never did that specific thing for me, but it emphasized that I am without someone to take care of me. Since it was at the end of the service, I just stayed until it was over, then I left quickly to make a clean getaway. I was having a hard enough time just keeping it together before getting to my car, and I didn't need anyone trying to engage me before I got there.

At some point, one of my friends extended a standing invitation for me to sit with her family any time I wanted/needed to, and I took her up on that for a time. I was very grateful to have an alternative to sitting alone.

As I began to heal, while I continued to be grateful for the support I had received from this community, I realized there was an element of obligation in my attendance. A lot of the families at church stepped up after Rod died. They came to the house. They brought me food and mowed my yard. They brought me money. They took care of Kristyn. They offered to take me places, to go with me to my mammogram, whatever. They got me through this tough time; my staying was a visible demonstration of my gratitude for all they'd done.

In that environment, I was part of a duo; we were Rod and

Gail. I was Rod's wife, and I desperately wanted to remain so. But I was changing. I did not like this person I was becoming for no other reason than she wasn't Rod's wife. I fought her arrival, and staying in a context where Rod's wife still existed made the fight easier.

It was somewhere in the third year after my loss that my attendance started to get increasingly spotty. I'd go to church for a few Sundays, then I'd miss one. Then I'd go for a couple of Sundays, then miss a couple. It got to where I'd go one Sunday and then miss three or four. There was one stretch where I missed six Sundays in a row. I remember counting. This pattern of more misses than hits made me feel more like a guest than a long standing member. And I eventually just stopped going to Sunday services in that third year.

It was also in this timeframe that my ideas about God were beginning to change, and I was becoming ideologically distanced from the teachings of my church. This added another element that made it easier for me not to be there.

It took me almost three years to the day to accept that I was no longer Rod's wife, that I no longer lived a life that included Rod doing the things that made me Rod's wife. It was time for me to accept this. I needed to be in a place where I could explore this new identity. Sadly, this church was not that place.

Even so, I tried my best during that time to maintain my connection to a community that I cared deeply for.

In that first year when I was invited to something, a women's Bible study for example, I would say I'd be there, fully intending on going when I said it. But getting ready to leave, or even pulling into the parking lot, I would just burst into tears, and I couldn't do it. At first I would call or text somebody that I knew was going to be there to let them know I couldn't make it.

Because I didn't like saying I was going to do something and then not doing it, I stopped saying Yes; I would just not commit to anything. And if it was something like working in the nursery where I was going to be depended on, I would tell them to plan on me not being there, but that if I was up to it at the time I'd show up and they'd have extra hands.

I felt flaky and unreliable. I didn't like being or even feeling that way. That's not who Rod's wife was.

So I started saying No to just about everything, even things I really wanted to participate in. But because I kept turning people down or rudely just not showing up, eventually I stopped getting asked. Mostly.

I remember confiding in one of my friends that when I say I'm going to do something, I have every intention of doing it. But when the time comes to do it, a lot of times I get overwhelmed and I just can't. I asked her to please continue to invite me to things and give me space to just show up if I can without committing ahead of time, allowing me to decide in the moment whether or not I could go. So she kept asking, and for that I am more grateful than she will ever know.

Even so, I watched many of my connections slowly erode as I drifted further and further from the life I shared with these friends, from the life I once lived.

Early on in my loss, for some of the harder days, I would go to Ryan and Glennda's church with them. They were still going to the same church they attended before Rod died, so this church walked with them through their grief. They had knowledge of Rod because Ryan shared his stories. Rod was known there – at least as a dad. When I visited there, I was Ryan's mom, not Rod's wife. I liked being at his church for this reason, but I never really considered going there on a regular basis.

Then in January of 2017, their church started a satellite campus at a new location, and Ryan and Glennda were both on the startup team. At that point, I hadn't been to my – or any – church for some months; the thought of going to a church where Rod never existed was almost as bad as staying at the church where I was still Rod's wife.

I decided I'd go support Ryan and Glennda on the Sunday of the soft-launch of their new campus.

As it so happened, his big brother and family were in town, so they came to the soft-launch. Kristyn came, too, and of course Ryan and Glennda were there – on the stage leading worship and in the nursery, respectively. Ryan did get to come sit with me for a bit during the message. I hadn't had this many of my kids in church with me in years, and I was loving it.

I connected with some people at the soft-launch, and I liked the pastor. But mostly I loved being in church with my kids. My oldest and his family would only be there for this one Sunday, and I wasn't gonna force Kristyn to go back to church, but at least I could be in church with Ryan and Glennda. So I went back the next week. And the next. I got involved in a small group and got to know some of the people a little better. So, yeah, this became my new church home.

Being back in a church environment every Sunday, in a place where Rod had never been, came with a mix of emotions from hopeful and excited to grief and sadness.

As difficult as it had become for me to be at C3, a benefit of being there was that I could just say something about when Rod did this Easter play or when he did that crazy thing at VBS and everyone would know what I was talking about. They could probably add their own memories to the story, too! But these new folks I was meeting didn't have that context or that history. And while some of them knew *of* Rod, they didn't know *my* Rod.

It was really odd the first time somebody asked me to tell them about him. I was like a deer in headlights – I had no idea what to say! I'd never had to tell somebody about Rod from a place of little to zero knowledge of him on their part.

I was with that little satellite campus until it closed after a couple of years, but the campus pastor started another church, called The Table, and I am still a member there.

Losing our church was hard, and I've had to grieve that loss. But it allowed me to try something different, and I like where I've landed.

THREE

Friends

"We all change, when you think about it,
we're all different people all through our lives,

and that's okay, that's good,
you've gotta keep moving,

so long as you remember
all the people that you used to be."

Doctor Who (TV series), "Time of the Doctor"

2013

I 4

⧉

Early Friendships

I went to the same schools with a whole lotta people from first through tenth grade. These were the kids I expected to graduate with, and probably the ones I would have kept in touch with after graduating. But life didn't happen like that for me.

We moved to another city (in another school district) in the last quarter of my sophomore year after my dad remarried, but I was allowed to finish my sophomore year before having to transfer into my new school district when school started in the fall.

I decided that I was not going to make any friends at this new school that year; it was merely a stop-over, a one year speed bump in my primary education journey. As a senior, I would be allowed to cross district lines and go back to my old stomping grounds and graduate with the people I'd journeyed with since the beginning.

Well, that was the plan, anyway.

In my junior year – that one year speed bump – I met Rod. So much for my no-new-friends policy! But choosing to spend time with him meant that I had less time to spend with friends from my old school, and I began to lose touch with all but a very few. And when the time came to enroll in my old school for my senior year, I decided to stay at my new school instead. So I graduated with this new group of kids that I'd only known for a couple of years. Those friendships didn't have the history I had with my other friends, and most of them were in the context of Rod. (I see the beginning of a pattern here ...)

I went to a state college starting the fall after I graduated from high school. I commuted to the campus in a nearby city; I arrived for my first class at 8:00 am, and I was on campus til my back-to-back classes were over at noon. Then I went to work at a clerical job I got for the summer where I worked from 1:00-5:00 pm, and homework and wedding planning came in the evenings after work. Without the convenience of living in a dorm (or even near campus), and with everything else I had going on outside of school, I had little to no time to make friends and have all those college experiences I'd always heard about.

I dropped out of college during my second year and got a clerical job in the loan processing department of a large US bank. Rod was going to a different college; he went a semester or two longer than I did before he quit and got a job stocking inventory for a clothing chain, which eventually led to him working for EDS, a large computer consulting firm in Texas.

At that point, our work friends became our primary friend group. But these friendships were short-lived ...

When we were 23 and our oldest was a year old, EDS moved us from California to Texas where Rod started his first official IT position. From that point on, everyone we would meet would meet us together, as a single family unit. We were Rod's wife, Gail's husband, or our kid's parents – all connected to one another, each one the context and reference points for the others. Rod and I were a couple, and we were known in this new place as such. Nobody here ever knew us apart from each other.

Within the next three years, we had a second son, started going to church, and I quit my job to be a full-time house-wife and mom. Without work friends, my friends were pretty much other women from church – most of whom were mar-ried, and had some kids.

Rod started teaching the Young Marrieds Bible Study class. Though they were a little younger than Rod and I, we all became friends. We all shared the context of married life.

Because of this shared context, I believed we, as wives, all operated from the same WIFE handbook. We knew to check the family calendar before making plans. We understood that dinner time was family time, so evening get-togethers automatically took that into consideration – accommodation for kids, affordability of a suggested restaurant for a larger family, and so on. Even girl's-nights were made with consid-erations – who would watch the kids, did dinner have to be prepared for the rest of the family before we went out, etc. Weekends had their own considerations – kids' sports prac-tices or events, music recitals, home repairs/improvements, date night, whatever other activities were all scheduled for (or relegated to) the weekends.

According to this 'married with children' handbook I had in my head, I believed we all understood what went into planning a group social activity, even small ones, like three or four ladies going to a movie together. We had much in common, though the details differed from one family to the next. We all knew the drill and followed our 'married-with-children' cultural norms.

<h1 style="text-align:center">15</h1>

Changing Friendships

In the weeks and months following Rod's death, my girl-friends were amazing. They put their own families and routines on hold so they could comfort and support me. They made themselves available to me – just a text away – whenever I needed them. They continued to include me in all the usual things – small group meetings and lunches, women's events, and the like – and they checked in with me when I was missing from regularly scheduled church activities, including Sunday morning services. For all these things and more I will be forever grateful. It was evidence that there was something in my life that hadn't ended.

With the support of my friends, I was able to move through life with some semblance of normalcy; it felt somewhat like a continuation of what life had been before Rod died. Continuing to participate in things with the people Rod and I shared our lives with was, indeed, comforting.

As the fog of my widow brain began to lift, I began to notice everyone sitting next to their sweeties – whether I was at a small group meeting in someone's home, at church, in a restaurant or almost anywhere else – except for me.

There is a particular lunch after church that I remember vividly.

Our Life Group (as we called our small groups at church) went to lunch together once a month after Sunday service. After a couple of months of hibernation, I decided it was time to get back into 'normal' life, and this was a safe place to take that first step.

For this particular lunch, the group decided to try out a newly opened Vietnamese restaurant just across the street from our church. It was one of those where you place your order at the register, get a number to take to your table, and they bring your order to your table when it's ready.

Rod liked Vietnamese food. The only time I had it was a work lunch we both went to. I had no idea about any of this food, so I trusted Rod to order something for me that I'd like. We'd been married long enough for him to know what I would and wouldn't eat. I don't remember what he ordered, but I do remember enjoying it.

This time there was no one who knew my tastes well enough to suggest something I would most likely enjoy. I stood in the line as all the couples in my group discussed the menu items pictured on the wall-mounted menu between themselves. I stood there, looking at the same menu they were talking about, but it was like looking at a foreign language. I fought back tears. I asked one of the men near me about a dish that I thought I might like. He described it to me, and I decided to give it a try.

I watched several couples ahead of me at the registers, him placing his order then she hers. The first couple that completed their order looked for a table large enough for our group. They settled on a row of tables for four with a single long bench seat on one side. Being the first to the table, they seated themselves across from one another on one end. The next couple followed suit. When I got to the table, I took the next available seat on the bench, and the couple after me took their place beside me, across from one another.

I stared for what seemed like an eternity at the empty chair across from me, fighting back tears again. I could hear the sounds of others around me, but that empty chair across from me screamed so loudly, it seemed to drown out everything else, leaving me face to face with another facet of Rod's absence.

One husband who landed somewhere down the row got up to get some napkins from the counter. When he returned, he sat in the chair across from me instead of across from his wife. He was undaunted by my this-close-to-ugly-crying face. He smiled at me, and asked generally of those in earshot what everyone had ordered.

As others were engaging in conversation, I noticed that the rest of the couples after that were scattered in with each other as they arrived at the tables. Instead of following the unspoken couples seating arrangement, the couples mixed in with one another across the tables, sorting plates as confused servers attempted to bring them to their rightful diners.

After a few minutes, my eyes met the eyes of the angel

who sat across from me in the empty chair for just a moment. He smiled and gave a slight nod, enough to let me know that he had seen me – my lostness, my aloneness in this group of long-time friends. He didn't draw attention to me, except to bring me out of my void and back into the world of the living.

I am so very grateful to him for that simple understated gesture. It meant the world to me.

This wasn't the only time something like that happened.

Our small group at our church wasn't designated specifically as a couples group; we all just happened to be married. Having that in common helped us know how to best support one another.

At our meetings, we'd mingle and munch first, then for the meat of the meeting we'd all end up sitting next to our spouses. It just naturally happened that way and it was fine.

After our group lunch at the Vietnamese restaurant, I noticed a change in where we all landed at our small group meetings – the seating became more random. This behavior was a change in our group dynamic, and I believed it was because of me.

They did it in a way that didn't cause me to feel like I was a problem, or a burden or an inconvenience. While I greatly appreciated it because it minimized the emphasis on the empty chair, I wasn't fond of the idea that a whole group of folks changed the way they interacted with one another because of me. I love them for seeing me, but this change wouldn't have happened, or even been necessary, if it weren't for me, and I didn't think it fair for them to change the whole group for me.

The problem then arose for me that in that environment, regardless of seating arrangements, that Rod's absence was still present. While I was starting to get used to the idea of him being gone at home, the fact that he was no longer part of another environment that we used to share was like a whole new loss. Like at the Vietnamese restaurant, it was a reminder of an absence that I hadn't realized until I was there.

As time went on, it became increasingly difficult for me to be with our couple friends – in small group activities or otherwise. When we got together, I felt like I was the odd man out. Much like holidays when all my kids are together, the fact that we were all there highlighted the fact that we *weren't all* there. Over time, I didn't find as much comfort and solace in being around our friends as I had before.

I found myself between a rock and a hard place. I didn't want to be responsible for causing others to alter the way they interact with one another. They shouldn't have to wonder whether or not they could hold hands or sit next to each other when I was around. I didn't want people adjusting their behaviors to accommodate me – I did not expect them to, and I didn't think that was fair to them.

But, on the other hand, seeing couples together magnified the fact that I was no longer part of a couple. That was difficult to bear, too.

I had no desire to abandon my friends. Many of these friendships were well-seasoned, and there was love and trust built into them. So I decided I'd try a different approach; instead of continuing in our small group, I would focus on women's events. This seemed a good solution; since there were no husbands at these events, there wouldn't be an empty chair where Rod should have been. We were just a group of women, and I thought it would be a good way for me to stay connected with my girlfriends while not being around couples.

So I started attending the ladies bible study. As expected, no men. That was by design, and it was great ... at first.

It didn't take long for me to realize that a lot of the topics of these bible studies have to do with marriage and family. But even if the topic was focused on Christian character as an individual believer, the application of those principles usually impacted those closest to us, including our husbands.

I found that husbands were still very present even though they were not physically there. Conversations were typically about things going on in our lives *in real time* – whether it was our kids (going off to college, getting married, having babies or moving across the country), or beginning to talk about our aging parents and how to navigate those changes; husbands were often part of these real-time conversations. I found that my contribution to these conversations had become exclusively past tense, and Rod slipped a little further into the past with each one.

I remember a discussion at one of these women's Bible studies. One of the younger women shared about a particular struggle she and her husband were having. It was one that Rod and I had wrestled with early in our marriage, so I shared our experience with that struggle. Since I had experienced and resolved a similar situation, I thought perhaps I could help, or at least encourage her that it could be resolved. Of course, I talked about Rod because we struggled with – and resolved – it together.

It felt like the conversation changed after that. The ladies seemed to feel less free to speak what was on their hearts. From my perspective, the environment was no longer safe for them because they had become aware of my emotions. I'm so grateful for their mindfulness of me, but I didn't want to be the reason someone had to hold their tongue and not get the support or encouragement she needed from the group. Once again, I felt I had changed the dynamic of the group, so I eventually stopped attending the women's Bible studies.

But there were other women's events I participated in, including a weekend women's retreat. We had some down-time after lunch on Saturday, and I was visiting with a group of ladies. Mind you, now, these were the women who I'd been friends with for years, who knew Rod just like I knew all their husbands, and who I had been doing life with.

They were all talking about past experiences with their husbands and telling funny stories. Well, Rod wasn't here now, but that doesn't negate the 30+ years that we had before, so I piped in with a funny story. We all laughed, just as I expected. It was what happened next that I didn't expect.

Once the laughter waned, each of the ladies decided to head back to their cabins to get some water or grab their Bible. Or they wanted to sit by the lake a while or catch a cat-nap before the next session. One by one, everyone left. I realize that this may have been a total coincidence, that it was just a natural break in the conversation, but it didn't feel like that at the time.

I thought, *Wow, talking about Rod is definitely a conversation killer.* So I learned real quick that it was not ok for me to talk about Rod.

In my heart, I don't believe that there was malice or anything negative behind their dispersing. It just happened. But, at the same time, it felt like talking about Rod changed the dynamic of the conversation, even if it was a funny story, one they knew and could have even added to.

I don't know. Maybe hearing me talk about Rod made them miss him. Maybe it reminded them that they might one day be speaking about their own husband only in the past tense. Maybe it was a little bit of both. Or maybe it was a complete coincidence.

Whatever the reason, I began to guard my words so that I didn't make everyone else uncomfortable, so that I didn't kill the conversation, you know? But then it was like everybody forgot about him, like he was being erased.

As far as the larger community goes, our church was my place of serving, learning, connecting, and relating; this was my community, these were my people. We served together, played together, cried together – we did life together. They were my people; we had a shared context. But when Rod died, my ticket into the married world expired, changing my context. Everything got ... messy.

I found myself a widow in a community of married people. But it was my context that was different, not theirs. For a while, I continued interacting in the same way that I always had. And that was fine at the time because I desperately wanted things to stay the way they always had. Besides, I still *felt* married, so there's that.

In Sunday morning services, I tried my best to find my new place in this congregation that Rod and I had been part of and served together in for nearly a decade. For a time, I sat with a friend and her family. I know she was genuine in inviting me to sit with them, and I felt loved and seen. But I couldn't help feeling that that wasn't my place; I wasn't – or felt I shouldn't be – her responsibility.

There was a small contingent of single women in our predominantly married congregation. Once or twice, I got to be brave enough to ask them if I might sit with them. I felt very welcomed, but I was still living in the married mindset. I didn't feel single, so I didn't feel like I belonged there, either.

Some Sundays, I sat alone, remembering what it was like to sit next to Rod and how our family took up a whole row. *That* was my place in *this* church – next to Rod.

Before and after many Sunday services, my interactions had been reduced to a quick hello or a 'drive-by' hug – quite likely because I was the one 'driving by.' When my attendance at church became spotty, a handful of friends continued to check in with me; for this I am ever so grateful.

I did not expect my friends to drop everything and come to my aid indefinitely and to keep their lives on hold for me. Just because my world had changed entirely didn't mean theirs did, nor should it. After a time, I chose not to interrupt their routine or their families with my ongoing journey to figure myself out and this new reality I found myself in.

I was slowly realizing that much of the commonality I had with my friends was based on what I saw as our shared context as wives, and trying to continue to live in that married mindset was breaking me. I was a widow now, with a completely new set of rules. But none of us knew what those new rules were; I was making it up as I went along. **I was changing, adapting to a life I had only ever observed from afar.**

In my experience of being on the outside of someone else's grief, I know how awkward it was for me. I didn't know what to say to my best friend whose baby was stillborn. I didn't want to "remind" her of her loss. I made innocent comments in general conversation that upset her. As it was not my intention to hurt my grieving friend, I chose to guard my words. Guarding my words became not using them, and that created distance between us – which I saw as being for her benefit – to ensure there were no further faux pas on my part. I believed she needed space to grieve, so I stepped aside, fully intending to pick back up with her when she was ready.

I wonder if my friends may have experienced a similar conundrum, being on the outside of my grief.

I know, beyond the shadow of a doubt, that my friends did their best for me, just as I believed I was doing for my friend. Everything they did (or did not do) was out of a genuine love for me. I understand that, and I love them for it. But I had to figure out what my new context was going to look like. What was it like to live in this world as a widow? What would Christmas be like now? How does widow exist on a Tuesday? I had to think about these things because this was my new context.

But because I didn't expect my friends to understand my new context, I started to keep them at arm's length. I knew enough to know that the only way for anyone to understand this context was to live it, and I wouldn't wish that on any of them. So I began to feel disconnected from my community, from my friends.

I continued on my widow journey – what choice did I have?

A couple of years into this new life, I was beginning to get an idea of what it's like to live as a widow. I was adjusting to this new context, to my new reality.

I stopped crying when I was driving home from work or school, and I could just come home instead of hoping someone would text me to go grab a bite to eat or even a cup of coffee. I started being able to prepare meals for one. The things that made me cry at the beginning, that upset me miserably, that just threw in my face that he wasn't here any more, I was able to move through without that incapacitating sadness.

As I learned how to live as a widow, I found myself less dependent on my friends.

In our culture, as I've experienced it, we are largely grief illiterate – we don't know what it looks like, how long it lasts, or how to live with it or to be with someone who is living with it. We seem to have this expectation that whenever you're done grieving, things will get back to 'normal.' So folks step back, create space for the grieving person to do their grieving, expecting to step back in and pick up where they left off. I believed this, too, feeling confident that my friends would be there, waiting for me on the other side.

The trouble is that I didn't know how much about me would change. My perspective changed – my priorities, how I navigate my days, what I believe about God and the meaning of life. So when the fog of grief lifted, there was no picking up where we left off. Their friend who entered the valley of the shadow of death died with Rod; a different person would emerge. Grief changed me from the inside out. And this new person no longer shared the common ground that we once did.

It's my world that changed, not theirs, and I do not expect them to change their world to accommodate me.

For as long as I can remember, it was my responsibility as a woman to make sure everyone else was comfortable. And I fully embraced the Christian ideal that a person should prioritize Jesus first, Others second, and Yourself last in order to find true J.O.Y. So that's what I did.

As I understood it, putting others first meant it was up to me to change/rectify it if someone was uncomfortable around me, regardless of whether or not I was responsible for their discomfort. If someone was sad, I was to cheer them up. If they were angry, it was on me to help calm them down. If they were afraid or scared, I needed to make them feel safe.

If I perceived that others were uncomfortable around me, it was up to me to make accommodation for them by changing my behaviors in an effort to alleviate their discomfort.

In regards to my widow journey, if talking about Rod or about my grief, my changing views of God, etc., made others uncomfortable, then I must not talk about these things. If living in a way that reflects my healing and my adapting to a different way of living makes someone uncomfortable, I must adjust my behaviors to meet their expectations so that they will be comfortable.

For example, when I perceived our small group dynamic

was changing because of me, it was up to me to alleviate the necessity for this change by removing myself. When I thought that my presence made it unsafe for other ladies in the bible study to share their burdens, it was my duty to correct that problem. I accommodated event planners by not committing to attend events that I very much wanted to attend. And so on.

So I continued following the narrative by not leaning too heavily on my friends for support after the "acceptable" length of time for grieving was completed. They were busy being responsible for their own selves and families, and didn't need the added burden of carrying another person's burden who society had deemed able to carry their own burden.

This manifested in my allowing (or creating) distance between myself and my friends and the expectations I put on them about being available for me. Taking responsibility for myself, I believed, meant being less dependent on them and pulling myself up by my bootstraps, as they say, figuring out this widow thing by and for myself.

In my new context as a widow, and with my current understanding of God, the idea of being responsible for myself means something very different than my previous understanding of this narrative. It's not about not being a burden to others, or being dependent on friends; those are external factors, focused on others.

Personal responsibility is understanding what is actually mine to control and being responsible for those things, and discerning what is not mine to control – not my responsibility – and letting go of those things.

Here are a few things that are within my control that I am taking responsibility for:

- My words and actions, and decisions about what I wear, where I go, etc.
- Living up to my own expectations and standards.
- My own happiness and comfort.

Things that are beyond my control, that I am no longer taking responsibility for:

- The opinions of others about my words, actions, appearance, activities, etc.
- Living up to the expectations or standards of others.
- The happiness and comfort of others.

As I am learning to be responsible for myself in these and other ways, I am growing in self-confidence. I'm finding it very freeing to let go of feeling responsible for the expectations or comfort of others. I don't ignore these things, but when it comes to bearing responsibility for them, I find that bearing only what is mine to bear is a much lighter burden to bear.

I had lunch with a friend a few years after Rod's death. I'd only seen her a handful of times since his memorial service. During our lunch, we talked about this and that, catching up with each other's lives as they were at that time. As I was talking about what was going on in my life, which included adjusting into life after Rod, I noticed she was tearing up. Curious as to what I said that could have made her sad, I realized it was because I had been talking about Rod. She listened quietly to the rest of my story, and then we were both quiet for a few moments.

Finally, with tears still in her eyes, she asked me something about Rod. I don't remember the question now; it was something I had already worked through, so I was able to answer her without getting upset or emotional.

I am so glad that she asked her question, though. She may not have realized that she needed to talk about how Rod's death impacted her, and having the discussion that followed helped her process that. Her tears, and the conversation that followed, were precious to me because it was evidence that Rod had not been completely erased from this world. She remembered him, and how he impacted her life. I'd much rather share tears of remembrance than feel like he's been forgotten.

On separate occasions and each in their own words, I had two women tell me that they couldn't imagine their life without their husband. They told me that every time they saw me, they were reminded of their possible future – a future they don't want to think about, much less live. All they could manage was to observe me from a distance to see what that life might look like.

Our collective worst nightmare of a possible future had become my present reality. I couldn't hide it, I couldn't escape it. I couldn't pretend to still be married. I was sad to see these relationships fade into the background, but I didn't want every interaction with them to be underscored with sadness – mine and theirs – the present moment being overtaken by a sense of looming death.

Seeing old friends after not seeing them for a good bit of time was sometimes ... awkward.

I believe the depth of grief is tied to the emotional investment in the person or relationship. Because I was fully invested in Rod, I had been experiencing all of these moments and emotions every day and processing them as they happened. Friends, co-workers and others who knew Rod, whose emotional investment was commensurate with their relationship with him, might not have had as many opportunities to process their grief as I did. So seeing me after some time had passed may have been one of those moments for them when they become consciously aware of the impact of Rod's absence. I don't believe they forgot that Rod died, but life had returned to normal for them. Seeing me after some time might bring up unexpected memories for them, much like when my phone would ring and thought it was Rod. Or when I got out four slices of bread when making my lunch for work. Or those moments when I could have sworn that I heard his office door open, or his slippered feet shuffling down the hall.

So if I hadn't seen someone since Rod's service or it'd been some years later, they might not know that I had experienced some healing. I was managing things. I was staying healthy. I was finding joy in things. I was able to be happy and laugh.

On several occasions, I'd been told – in a very surprised way – that I looked good. I understand it was meant as a compliment, but what did they expect? A little black cloud hovering over an unkept, stooped figure all dressed in black? And given my belief about me being responsible for the comfort of others, I felt obligated to make them comfortable, and that typically meant putting on a mask and not living into my current state of healing.

It's been a journey, learning to live into this widow life; people may not be aware of my journey. The process is slow, and the changes are gradual but cumulative. Sometimes I wasn't even aware how much I'd changed until I connected with someone I hadn't seen for a while, and sometimes that felt a bit awkward to me.

But I am ready to embrace that awkwardness – to allow space for it in my world. It's my hope that pushing through the awkwardness will allow space for them to get to know who I'm becoming.

16

New Friendships

One challenge I've experienced in making new friends as a widow is knowing that people I meet now have never met Rod. The only thing they will ever know of Rod is what I tell them. They'll only ever know my understanding – my interpretation, my experience – of Rod, because that's all I have. I don't have his inner thoughts or his perspectives on things. They will only ever know my version of him.

Think of it this way. Two friends go see a movie together. If you ask each of them what they thought of the movie, you're probably going to get two different stories because each individual goes into the movie with their own life experiences and expectations. They are going to pick up on different nuances, and different things are going to stand out to each of them. Each person is going to relate to the characters and situations differently than the other. That's why you can have movie reviews where one reviewer says it was the best movie they've ever seen, and another one says they can't believe they paid money to see it – that they'll never get those two hours back. Same movie, different stories.

In a similar fashion, we experience people in light of our own experience, our own context; we see them through our own filters. If someone talks to my kids about their dad, they're going to get a different story from each kid, and their depictions of their dad will be different from the stories I tell of my husband. Rod was a multi-faceted human being, as we all are, and hearing only my story about him does not give a complete picture of who he was. It makes me sad to think that people I meet now will never see the whole picture, they'll never know who Rod really was.

I can't do much about people not knowing Rod. What I can do is be open enough to let them get to know me. They'll see glimpses of Rod in me (whether or not they are aware), and that'll have to be enough.

Being in a pandemic and locked down has given me time to explore some things and figure myself out. I am getting to the point where I am getting to know what I like to do and what I do for fun well enough to be able to have a meaningful conversation with new people I meet.

I have more confidence in myself, and I look forward to meeting people, learning about them and sharing with them who I am now. I feel like I know myself a little better now. I'm learning how to be friends with people as just Gail. So that's kind of where I am now.

Through this whole process, I've learned some things about what I believed to be true about friendships.

Much like I believed that love was based on need, I believed that friendship was based on context. Most of my friendships throughout my life – in high school, college, work, and church – reflect this belief. I am learning that this belief is just not true.

Now, the only qualification someone needs to be my friend is that they are a human being. Does that mean I will be 'besties' with every person I meet? Not necessarily, but it does mean that I won't disqualify anyone from being a friend because I can't see a shared context – like if they aren't my age or a widow, or if they hold different religious or political views, or live a different lifestyle than I live.

I watched a YouTube video (TV 2 | All That We Share) about people finding common ground. It starts by grouping people together within certain contexts (nurses, executives and working poor, former prisoners, ethnic and religious people, city- and country-folk, young and aged people, etc.) Then they ask the question, "Who in this room was the class clown?" People begin to smile, even laugh, as folks emerge from every group and come to the center of the room. Then, "Who is a step-parent?" Again, people emerge from different groups to join each other in the center. "Who has seen a UFO?" "Who loves to dance?" and so on. It ends with this statement, "So maybe there's more that brings us together than we think."

I've also realized that, as complex and multifaceted creatures, human beings have life experiences beyond what is visible to the world. To disqualify someone from being my friend because they don't currently share my context, beliefs, or lifestyle hardly seems fair. People are more than what they like to do, who they love, where they work, or what they believe.

People are ever changing. We haven't always been who or where we are today, and we will be different people in the future. Consequently, friendships will change, too.

I've learned to hold space for friends to be who they are. And I have gained the freedom to allow myself to live into my own changing views, life station or circumstance.

Growth of individuals in a friendship might be in tandem, or it may happen independently of one another. If one friend grows or changes beyond what the other friend can support, that doesn't necessarily mean that that friendship is over for good. Both individuals are capable of growth, and it's possible for friends to circle back around, and an estranged friendship can be renewed.

The caveat I've learned is that, if that happens, I am best served by putting aside any old expectations and approaching the renewing of an old friendship as though it was a new one. That doesn't mean forgetting what came before, wiping the proverbial slate clean; it means holding my pre-existing ex-perience of my old friend loosely, and observing the version of this person that is now before me – without comparing it to the version I knew before.

It would also serve me well to acknowledge that I am also a different version of myself than I was before, and to allow myself to live into who I am now. And maintaing a sense of humor couldn't hurt.

Another thing I've come to accept about friendships is

that they have their own life cycles, each one serving a purpose in the lives of both friends. Very few friendships last the duration of one's life. If you have one that does, treasure it, nurture it, for it is indeed a rare thing.

Losing Rod showed me that nothing on this earth is forever, no matter how much we want it to or believe it will be. **I have learned to accept that people will come and go throughout my life; I can choose to love them and enjoy their company while they're with me.** And when we've experienced all the things with one another that we were meant to experience, we can take our leave and continue our separate journeys. And that's ok.

In that in-between time – the space between longing for old friendships and forging new ones – I'm learning to be my own friend. Not so that I won't need friends, but so I can enjoy them and not expect from them things that I can find within myself.

FOUR

Traditions

"On the other hand,
our old ways were once new,

weren't they?"

Tevye, "Fiddler on the Roof" 1971

17

Thanksgiving

One year, when our kids were small, we headed out to spend Thanksgiving weekend with my best friend and her family, who lived about three hours south of us. My friend and I were up before dawn to prepare the turkey and get it in the oven. I remember the two of us laughing about how we got out of bed early for the privilege of sticking our hands into the turkey's business, and laughing even harder when that contact produced farting noises! Who knew two grown women would be so amused by a naked, farting turkey in the pre-dawn hours? Perhaps we were that tired. Or maybe we were both influenced by the three boys we were collectively raising. Anyway, we got that bird stuffed and in the oven, and we went back to bed for a bit.

This memory stands out to me because it stands in stark contrast with how I typically spent Thanksgiving morning with just our family.

I would get up (after the sun!) and watch the Macy's Thanksgiving Day Parade, still wearing my jammies. This parade has always held a special place in my heart. My mom worked at Macy's before I was born. Being a Macy's employee, she got a front row seat to the parade from an upper floor window – a bird's eye view of all the activities and an almost eye-level view of the balloons as they passed. I don't have much more than this single image in my mind's eye, but even this small memory is a connection to my mom who passed away when I was 12. Watching the parade on Thanksgiving morning – seeing the floats, listening to the bands and watching the dance numbers, oohing and aahing at the horses and laughing at all the characters walking and cycling along between the floats, and cheering when Santa makes his grand entrance at the end of the parade – feels like inviting her into my day and actively (if silently) including her in my gratitudes.

Most years, at least one of my kiddos, and sometimes Rod, would join me in watching from the beginning, but everyone was usually on the couch with me by the time Santa arrived on his sleigh. That was my cue to begin Thanksgiving dinner preparations!

Once I was in the kitchen, the sounds of the house changed. High school bands, pop singers, and Christmas songs were replaced with the sounds of cheering crowds and practiced announcers narrating whatever football game was being aired ... and Rod found them all! I followed the various games via the announcers' narrations and Rod's exclamations, joyous or otherwise.

I'd begin by preparing the turkey, giggling to myself as

I stuffed it remembering the early morning encounter with my friend. I'd plan an oven schedule around the turkey's designated cook time, preparing our candied sweet potatoes and green bean casserole so they'd be ready to go into the oven when the turkey came out. While the turkey cooked, I'd sit and watch football with my sweetie. But once the turkey was done and out of the oven, it was a mad dash until we all sat down at the table together to enjoy our feast and one another. I did all the cooking, but it was something I enjoyed doing.

Oh, in case you were wondering, there were pies, usually prepared and cooked the day before. We started out with only two: apple pie, which was Rod's favorite, and cherry pie, which was mine. The kids liked one or the other (or both), so everyone was happy. But our little dessert menu grew along with our family; pumpkin and non-fruit pies became part of our tradition as we added daughters-in-law to our family.

After our two oldest had moved into their own places, Rod and I still hosted Thanksgiving dinner for all of us. Like our dessert menu, our traditions continued to grow, expanding with the needs of our family. While others began bringing their own contributions to our now community dinner, I still loved handling the bulk of the cooking. I was honored, and it was my pleasure to serve all these human beings I called family.

I didn't give much thought to Thanksgiving the year Rod died. I had been completely focused on taking care of Rod for most of the year. When November rolled around, Rod was in pretty rough shape. He'd gone from about 160 at the beginning of the year down to 120 pounds. He had very little appetite, and he couldn't eat much when he did manage to eat. He was very weak, and he slept a lot. I honestly don't remember if I even had any conversations with anyone about Thanksgiving dinner.

On Monday, November 18, Rod was taken by ambulance to the hospital after throwing up what looked like coffee-grounds during the night. With IV fluids and medical care, he began to feel a little bit better. The internal bleeding seemed to stop, and we talked about getting handicap rails installed in the house, particularly in the bathroom. But we did not talk about Thanksgiving, which was the following week.

On Wednesday, the 20th, they moved him to ICU following an EUS (endoscopic ultrasound). They discovered that the tumor was pressing into the duodenum, causing the over-stretched skin of his small intestine to bleed. There was nothing they could do to stop it. It was possible that the wound could scab over on its own, but there was nothing preventing the tumor from exerting force and causing it to tear again. They were just trying to keep him comfortable.

The next day, his oncologist told me that Rod would prob-ably not recover from this.

The holiday celebrating gratitude that was eight days away was still not on my radar.

On Friday, the 22nd, right around evening shift change, they moved Rod from ICU to the cancer floor of the hospital. It was in this cold, dark room, just before midnight, that I said good-bye to the love of my life, my soul-mate, my best friend, my world.

Time stopped.

Only Kristyn was with me. I called my boys; they arrived after Rod had already died. I wanted to call them sooner, but I knew that Rod wouldn't have wanted them to see him like that. If he was aware that Kristyn was there, I'm pretty sure he was not happy about that for just that reason.

We stayed in the room with him for a while after he died, being joined by the friend who I'd been having dinner with in the hospital earlier, when they moved Rod to the cancer floor. My friend packed up the few things they brought with Rod from the ICU, things she had helped unpack just a few hours before.

The kids left one by one and headed to my house. The hospital staff told me I could stay longer, that they would notify me when the funeral home was about to arrive. I took them up on that. My friend stayed with me until I left, and she walked me to my car then followed me to my house. We were up until we started to see sunlight coming through the windows, then I fell asleep on the couch.

The calendar said Saturday, but I seemed to be existing outside of the calendar. For me, it was a non-day.

Out-of-town family and friends began to arrive over the next few days to share stories, grieve together, and attend services.

Thanksgiving briefly entered my consciousness as we made arrangements, but only in the context of whether or not I wanted out-of-town family and friends to have to contend with last minute flights on a major holiday, possibly missing their own family celebrations. And since I was leaving for Israel four days after Thanksgiving and not returning until mid-December, I didn't want to delay services. So we scheduled them – a graveside for family and celebration service for everyone – for Tuesday, November 26.

On Wednesday, the 27th, some wonderful folks from church brought a complete, fully cooked Thanksgiving meal to the house. It was enough to feed all of us, including guests who were still in town. I am grateful to them for bringing some form of normalcy to this topsy-turvy world, but I don't even remember eating any of it. I honestly don't remember much about that Thanksgiving Day. It didn't exist for me. While I was functioning in the 'real' world, I was existing outside of time.

The rest of the Thanksgiving weekend, I was focused on packing for my trip. A good friend, who had traveled to Israel before, and would be going on this trip with me, came to the house and helped me pack and create a list of things I'd need to get before leaving the following Tuesday.

Thanksgiving didn't happen for me in 2013. It just didn't exist for me. I was numb, just going through the motions, just trying to remember to breathe.

By the next Thanksgiving (2014), Kristyn and I had moved to a new (to us) house. That fact alone meant Thanksgiving was going to be different. There were no memories of Thanksgiving dinners in this new kitchen – of it being crowded with family and food and laughter. No memories of watching the Macy's Thanksgiving Day parade or hearing football games in the background. Thanksgiving had not existed for us in this new place. It was a clean slate; there were no memories of Rod in this place. Thanksgiving as I had known it was now relegated to memory with no physical cues to remind me of what had been.

There had been a particular way to spend the day, from an expected menu to prescribed dialogues that were 'supposed' to take place on that day. I found I was no longer able to fulfill any of the traditional expectations of the day in a normal or meaningful way. The kids all still came to the house and there was food, but it was different. Even though it looked familiar.

It wasn't even like I was trying to fit a square peg into a round hole – there was no freaking hole! I was left standing there, with my little square peg, on the edge of a place where there used to be … something. That something was big, and it was taken away from me, leaving a void in its place.

Realizing that there would not be a new place to fit my square peg, I decided it was time to set that peg down and reimagine what Thanksgiving might look like for me going forward. I tried some new things – from preparing the whole shebang again to cooking a regular family meal; from inviting friends over for a FriendsGiving dinner to spending the day with just my kiddos to spending it just me and Kristyn and a good old fashioned Twilight Zone marathon.

I haven't settled on a new tradition. Perhaps I don't need to.

Instead of focusing on the *activities* of a single day designated to giving thanks, what if I focused on *gratitude itself*?

Gratitude is a mindset. It's a way of viewing the world and everything in it, And it's a mindset I can choose to have every day, not just every fourth Thursday of November.

And if I chose gratitude every day, then do I really need a day to remind me to be grateful? No, I don't.

What about sharing what I'm grateful for with others? Once again, I can do that any time I'm with … anyone.

So I'll choose to live gratefully every day. I'll express my gratitude towards others as I encounter them. And on that designated day in November, I'll enjoy a meal – whether turkey with all the trimmings or a big pot of spaghetti – with whoever happens to be journeying with me on that day. Easy-peasy. I think I like the sound of that.

18

Christmas

Over the course of my lifetime, I have participated in a number of different Christmas traditions.

As a little girl, I was allowed to sleep in my big brother's room on Christmas Eve. I'd get my indoor sleeping bag and lay it out on the floor beside his bed. Of course, there wasn't all that much sleep that went on, but any antics were from our respective sleeping spots and quiet enough to not be heard outside of his room. Baba (my toddler version of his name that stuck) would let his hand hang from under the bottom of his blankets to become "Spidey." I'd giggle and swat at Spidey who would immediately run back up his "web" and out of my sight. Then I'd eagerly anticipate his return, my gaze moving up and down the length of the blanket not knowing from whence he would emerge next.

At first light, we invaded our parents' bedroom, jumping on their bed in our excitement to open our presents.

Mom made sure we started with breakfast, then we'd open all the presents that Santa left under our tree. We'd have only a few minutes to play with our new toys before we had to get dressed. For me that meant a frilly (usually velvet or sateen) Christmas dress, tights, and patent leather shoes. While I loved the idea of dressing up, this was not the best outfit for a little girl to play in – and keep clean, run-free, and unscuffed.

Next, we headed to my aunt and uncle's house for lunch and more presents. With five cousins already in the house, the environment was chaotic, and it took longer for everyone to eat and open all their presents. We'd have only a few minutes to play with the new toys we got there before we all had to leave and head over to our grandparents' house for dinner and ... you guessed it, more presents.

This last stop seemed to be the main event of the grown-ups' day. My Nana and Popi's house was not big, but, in addition to the 11 of us arriving en masse, there was usually a crowd already gathered, with more arriving after us – mostly extended family on Nana's side that I only ever saw at her house on Christmas Day. While I only had one aunt and uncle, my mom had at least three or four within driving distance, and all of them had kids. I gave up trying to figure out how everyone was related and just figured that every-one there was someone's cousin. It was loud, crowded, full of stories and great food.

Speaking of food, Nana and Popi started cooking the day before, producing more food than it seemed their tiny kitchen should be able to produce. It was mostly a traditional Spanish spread, including paella and eggplant parmesan. They had a large covered patio with rows of tables, set with festive tablecloths and place settings, which were pushed to the side to allow space to mingle and dance after the meal. There were people everywhere – they filled the little house and spilled outside of it, into both the front and back yards – everyone laughing, crying, and catching up with one another.

After an exhausting family-filled day, we'd return home, too tired to even remember all the presents we'd opened that day, nevermind having the energy to play with any of them. This was my childhood Christmas tradition.

Rod and I spent our first few Christmases with each other, and with our families of origin. Three years into our marriage, Rod's job moved us halfway across the country – from California to Texas – where we settled in with our 1-year-old. Our first Christmas away from our families was difficult, to say the least. I was homesick – and pregnant. Not a good recipe for a memorable, happy holiday. All I could focus on was what wasn't.

Neither Rod nor I had a Christmas experience growing up that didn't involve multiple stops and lots of family. It was strange, just the three of us, but we kept up what traditions we could. We put up our little tree, letting the toddler help with ornaments, and we got a new lighted star that Rod put atop the tree. I cooked a modest meal of just our favorite Christmas foods. It was quite simple, and very quiet (despite the toddler).

With nowhere to go on Christmas Day, we just stayed in our pajamas all day. We started late and took our time, opening one present at a time and allowing time between presents for our little one to actually play with the new thing until he was ready for the next one. While quite without intention, this would become a family tradition, one that was birthed in the void of what had been. It was an adaptation to a new life for our little family that had been flung so far from its roots. That little change created space for a string of new traditions that would develop in the coming years – many of which were quite intentional – that would become part of our own family culture.

The next Christmas we were four. We were settled into our new locale and jobs and without raging pregnancy hormones, we were set up for a better Christmas. And it was, indeed, better than the one before.

Over the years, we added Christmas Eve traditions, too. Everyone would open up one present (of course, they were all new jammies so we looked good for photos in the morning). We'd all change into our new pjs, then pile into the car to go look at Christmas lights. Wearing pjs made it easier for us to carry sleeping kids straight to their beds when they were little. When they got a little older we added having a cup of hot cocoa together between looking at lights and going to bed. We'd get the sleeping room ready, whether Kristyn was joining her brothers (who shared a room) or big brothers got to crash with their baby sister. Remembering my adventures with my own big brother, I had no illusion about what would go on after we shut the door; Rod and I were ok with it, as long as the volume was reasonable and that door didn't open. This last thing was imperative.

Once the kids were in bed – and presumably asleep – that's when "Santa" showed up at our house! Rod and I would gather all the kids' presents that we'd been accumulating and hiding all over the house for the past couple of months. Rod would take care of any assembly that needed to happen (i.e. bicycles), then he would join me in wrapping everything else until it was all done and everything was under the tree. Then we'd finally go to bed. The older the kids got, the later they stayed up, and so did we! But given that they were older and we had nowhere else to be on Chrtistmas morning, we got to sleep in a bit.

Over the years, our Christmas traditions continued to grow until it had become our own unique collection of experiences for and with our own kids; things they would hopefully look forward to, and, later, the stories our children would tell.

We started from scratch when we moved away from our own family traditions, and we created new ones that continued to grow and adapt with our family.

Eventually it was just me, Rod, and Kristyn on Christmas Day. The first year that the boys and their families came over to do our usual Christmas morning thing on Christmas Eve, we opened *all* the presents, leaving the three of us feeling a little flat on Christmas morning. So we went to the movies.

Even though we had to change out of our pajamas, we decided that this would be the foundation of new traditions, ones that Rod and I could carry over to just the two of us once Kristyn moved out. Hey, we created something new after a complete upheaval of what was normal once before; we could do it again. I anticipated that we would build on our Christmas Day movie adventures, adapting and adding new traditions as our lives continued to change. Then, one day, decades from now, we'd marvel at what we'd built in this new life we were building together, just the two of us.

Rod and I had already reinvented Christmas once before, and we were ready to step into reinventing it again. We had a blank slate on which to create those new traditions back then.

But with Rod gone, there wasn't even a slate – blank or otherwise.

Christmas was only 33 days after Rod died (and 10 days after I got back from Israel), so Kristyn and I had to figure something out. I decided we should go ahead and put up the tree, if for no other reason than for the grandkids.

So, I went out to the garage to get the artificial tree and all its trimmings that we had used for decades. I opened the garage door, stared across the double garage at where the boxes were stowed. I stood in tearful silence, then backed out the door and closed it behind me. Nope. That wasn't going to happen.

So, Kristyn and I decided to get a real tree. We thought doing something completely different would be ... we didn't know what it would be. But we knew we couldn't do things the same. Because it wasn't the same.

We headed to our local Lowes on a cold and drizzly night just a week before Christmas and went into the live tree tent in the parking lot. I don't remember ever having a live tree before, so this was way out of our ballpark. But then we'd never had a Christmas without Rod before, so we were already out there.

We chatted with the staff and made our selection – a Douglas fir. We named him Douglas; it seemed appropriate.

They asked us what kind of car we had. My answer elicited looks of "Okay ... we can make that work." They wrapped Douglas up in a net and strapped him to the roof of my Lexus, and we headed home.

We arrived home, proud of ourselves for making all the decisions without melting down in front of anyone. And then we looked at Douglas atop my car, looked at the long walkway from the curb to the front door. Finally, we looked at each other questioning the wisdom of our decisions.

We probably looked pretty comical, unstrapping that 7' fir tree, rolling it off the car, and dragging it up to the door. Once we got it into the living room, we stared blankly at each other once again as we realized we had no idea how to get from a wrapped live tree laying on the floor to a fluffy upright tree standing in its little stand.

I'm not sure how we did it, but we got Douglas upright, fluffed out and watered – without killing him. Or ourselves. That was the last time we had a live tree.

We had coordinated with the boys and their families to open presents and celebrate Christmas together on New Year's Day, so that meant it was just me and Kristyn for Christmas morning. We decided that if it had been the three of us, we would have gone to see a movie like we had done for the last two years, so we went and saw The Secret Life of Walter Mitty.

Being so close to Rod's death, that Christmas was heavy with grief; I don't remember much else.

The next couple of Christmases were difficult, particularly when we were all together. Because we weren't all together. You know how when someone steps out of the room for a minute to get something from the kitchen or go to the bath-room but you know they're coming back, and there's a space where they were but no one fills it because they are coming right back? It was kind of like that. There was that space that no one would fill because it was Rod's space. But he wasn't coming right back; his space just remained empty. And when we were all together, his empty space was still there with us; his absence became more prominent when our whole family was present.

In the years following, Kristyn and I continued going to the movies on Christmas day (with two exceptions when my oldest was visiting from out of town) until the covid pandemic hit in 2020.

I continued to put up a tree almost every year, but it was mostly for my grandkids. With no grandkids coming to the house in 2017, Kristyn and I threw some lights on an artificial ficus we already had in the living room and called it a day. We were clearly still not in a place to celebrate Christmas. It took a couple more years for us to enjoy Christmas again.

A few years ago, we found ourselves a little disappointed when we finally took down the tree in early January, so we decided to put up our artificial tree around the first of October and decorate it with orange lights and Halloween ornaments. After Halloween, we switched to amber lights and Fall themed ornaments, and redecorate it once again after Thanksgiving with multi-colored lights and our old – and new – Christmas ornaments. We also decorate the house now – inside and some outside – with appropriately themed holiday decorations.

After doing this a couple of years, we found ourselves all the more disappointed when it finally came time to take it all down in January. So we redid the tree one more time with white lights and Poly-Fiberfill to create a winter tree covered in snow after we packed up all the Christmas decor. It stayed up until the weather started to feel like spring. That worked – we were ready for it to be put away by then.

I'm glad I've come back around to where I can enjoy the whole holiday season again. Rod will always be missed; he will always be part of my Christmas past. I am also creating new experiences that reflect where I am now in life, and who I am after Rod.

19

Easter

When our kids were little, Easter involved a good amount of preparation on the grown-ups' part. I'd shop for goodies for Easter baskets, and I'd boil eggs for the kids to decorate and/or stuff plastic eggs with candy. We'd all get new fancy outfits to wear to church – if I was going to be sewing any of them, I had to make this decision even earlier so I'd have time to get them all done!

On Easter morning, the kids would find their baskets on the counter when they came to breakfast, but they were only allowed one piece of candy before church. (Yes, this is the voice of experience talking.) When they were little, little, Rod and I would hide their eggs and they'd have an Easter egg hunt in the backyard before church. When they got a little older, we'd wait until after church, and some years the church would host a church-wide egg hunt for all the kids on the church grounds.

After church and any Easter-related activities afterwards, we'd head home and I'd get to cooking. Instead of a traditional Easter ham, we had a Hawaiian meal – kalua pig and rice. The preparation of this meal lent itself to being a community event as anyone could help shred the pork roast as we shredded it by hand.

As we became more involved in various ministries of our church, Rod and I found ourselves involved in the annual Easter plays. Rod was part of it in some capacity nearly every year, and played a variety of roles over the years, including Jesus. I usually helped with costuming or in some other behind-the-scenes role.

Rehearsals for these performances started at least a couple months before Easter, if not sooner, adding to our pre-Easter activities. Those rehearsals became more frequent (and dare I say more intense) with dress- and tech- rehearsals as we got closer to Easter.

In 2013, our church did an Easter play that Rod wrote, called "The Rehearsal." He directed it and played the lead – a janitor! – all while he had undiagnosed cancer. It was this play that delayed his diagnosis.

He hadn't been feeling well and had been losing weight since January; he assumed it was just some bug he couldn't shake. It didn't really start taking a toll on him until a month or so before Easter, and he felt he was too far into the production at that point to step out. So he decided he would go to the doctor after Easter, which was on April 1st that year; we got his diagnosis a week later.

After Rod died, I really struggled with the whole Easter/resurrection thing. Frankly, I was just over it. It didn't do me – or Rod – any good believing in the resurrection of Jesus as Rod laid there dying. That whole resurrection thing just seemed ... powerless. What good is all that power if God's not going to use it? Yes, I realize it's a story about our ultimate resurrection into heaven at some point in the future after our physical death, but if that's really all it's about, then why did Jesus raise Lazarus, Jairus' daughter, or the widow's son from the dead? Clearly, this power is literal and present; it's apparently also selective. And Rod wasn't selected. Resurrection became powerless, and Easter was empty.

Nevertheless, I continued attending Easter Sunday services somewhere – at least until the pandemic. I suppose it was more out of habit or obligation than anything else at that point.

As for other traditional Easter activities, it was only in the last couple of years (still during the pandemic) that there's been a grandbaby old enough to hide Easter eggs for; even that fell by the wayside this year. Being the last tradition standing, making kalua pig for our family meal now seems arbitrary.

Without all the tangible reminders repeating the biblical stories of Easter in my mind, my attention turned to the intangibles that had been running like an undercurrent in my soul. What is Easter really all about – beyond the story of Jesus on the cross? What does resurrection even mean, and what does a resurrection life look like? What does it look like for me?

I know all the traditional answers for these questions. Those have satisfied my intellect, my thinking for many years.

But those one-size-fits-all answers didn't satisfy any more. They just didn't reach my soul.

Ryan shared with me a conversation he had with Rod about the resurrection of Jesus, and about living a resurrection life. Rod was physically abused as a child, as was his dad; physical abuse was generational in his family line. While Rod consciously decided before we even got married that he would not abuse his kids, he had an experience when our oldest was about four years old that made him realize that he was, indeed, on the same path as his father, despite his desire and choice not to be.

Fast forward to 1997. Rod went on a short-term mission trip to Argentina with then Global Missions Fellowship, the non-profit he would become the IT Guy for three years later. Something happened in him on that trip that changed him, and he broke the generational cycle of physical abuse. While the mindset was immediate, the habit took longer to break. But he now had space in his own being, between the impulse and the action, that allowed him to choose how he would respond to his kids (who were 13, 11 and eight years old at that time) rather than be chained to the conditioned response of his lineage. He was finally able to honor his own decision not to abuse his kids.

He shared with Ryan that this is resurrection life – the ability to make a different choice every morning with the knowledge and confidence that he has the ability to follow through and stay on his chosen path. Every single day, he died to who he was before, and was resurrected as a new man, as the dad he always wanted to be.

Hearing this story allowed me to see what resurrection

meant for Rod. What might it look like for me? Easter is about resurrection, and resurrection is about the cycle of life, death, and rebirth. Curious, I wondered where else might I observe this cycle of life, death, and rebirth – other than the story about Jesus?

So I started paying attention.

There's a natural science museum and wildlife sanctuary that I love to visit. I especially love the trees, some of which are over 250 years old. Every fall, every leaf on those very old trees dies. They fall to the ground and are effectively buried as they decompose and become part of the soil. Then, like magic, every spring that very old tree sprouts very new leaves. Though the core or the essence of the tree didn't die, it has undergone and participated in a kind of death which was then followed by a kind of resurrection in all of its new leaves. If I go there every year, I am effectively seeing a different tree, though the core of it remains.

Likewise, many cells in the human body die off and new cells are birthed in a repeated and predictable cycle, some cells dying off in a matter of days or hours, others lasting up to a decade or longer. Our bodies are in a constant death and rebirth cycle. I am physically not the same person I was when Rod died ten years ago.

This death and rebirth process goes beyond the physical manifestation in our bodies. Any time a person dies to something, something else is born. Rod died to the generational cycle of physical abuse, and a new dad was born. There was no room for that new dad in that former, abusive version of himself; it wasn't until Rod died to his old way of thinking, of behaving, of living that he could be reborn. That's resurrection life.

The me I was with Rod died with him – my identity, my beliefs, life as I knew it. Once I allowed myself to die to that version of who I was, a new life was resurrected in me. Every time I die to some part of myself by letting go of an old belief or habit, I am reborn; I begin to walk in the newness of life (Romans 6:4). This is my resurrection life.

Resurrection is not a one-time event, it's not about a final destination. It's about the cycles of life, death, and rebirth that happen in and around us throughout our lives. I can find reminders of and have opportunities to witness and experience resurrection every day. It is the power to be reborn after everything has been destroyed.

So what does Easter look like for me now?

Well, Much like Thanksgiving became for me more about gratitude that can be lived every day than about what food I eat on a particular day, Easter is becoming more about living the resurrection life every day than about all the activity that used to surround it.

20

Other National Holidays

We didn't do anything in particular for some of the national holidays, like St Patrick's Day or April Fool's Day, so his absence didn't really impact these holidays for me.

Holidays like Memorial Day and Fourth of July were prime barbecue days. We didn't have specific traditions for days like these, but we usually did something. Sometimes Rod would barbecue for just our family, other times we had people over, or we'd share a community barbecue (i.e. a church event or a group of friends).

Watching fireworks on the 4th was hit or miss. To watch a fireworks display in person meant arriving before dark, finding a spot, and waiting until it was dark. In Texas in July, this was when the mosquitos were most active, and the gathering of sweaty people was an "all you can eat" buffet for them! And mosquitoes especially loved Rod and Kristyn. Yeah, that was enough for us to find other ways to watch fireworks. If we could find a fireworks show not too far away, we'd drive somewhere close enough to see them from our car, or sometimes Rod would get up on the roof of our house with the kids and see what they could see from there. I think because there wasn't a specific tradition associated with these holidays, the sting of his absence wasn't as sharp.

For Mother's Day, Rod usually got me a present (along with gifts from the kids) and we'd all go out to dinner, but neither of these were necessarily exclusive to Mother's Day.

The most difficult part of Mother's Day happened at church, oddly enough. I'm not sure exactly why that was – maybe the public "stand-up-if-you're-a-mom" the pastor called for and seeing the pride in the husbands' eyes as they honored their wives. Maybe it was hearing about (and/or seeing) all the wonderful gifts my friends received that morning from their husbands. While these things did sting, I think the biggest thing I felt was … annoyance. Since my kids were grown and Rod wasn't there to "honor" me during that part of the service, it all felt irrelevant to me in that setting. I knew cognitively that I am still my kids' mother, but they weren't even there! It felt odd, standing up with all the other moms but with no family there with me.

So I ended up at Ryan and Glennda's church for most Mother's Days. Their pastor did the same type of public acknowledgement things, but it felt different to me. I believe it was context – Rod was never in this environment. It was just my kids, and I was able to receive it as they honored me as their mom on Mother's Day.

Rod liked to barbecue on Father's Day, but even that was not a yearly event. I remember getting him a super nice charcoal grill in 2012, and he enjoyed barbecuing even more on that grill, the few times he did. That might have become an annual tradition, but we never got the chance to find out.

The hardest part of Father's Day for me was knowing that my kids were missing their dad.

Halloween was mostly for the kids. Once they'd grown up, our participation was down to getting candy to pass out to trick-or-treaters, then eating most of it before they came. There would occasionally be a Halloween party for us to dress up for and attend, but those events were few and far between.

In recent years, I have started to enjoy more things about Halloween, like dressing up just to pass out candy to the neighborhood kids, and especially to take my grandson trick-or-treating in my neighborhood! As I have loosened my grip on my prior religious beliefs, I feel like I have permission to actually enjoy some of the fun this holiday has to offer.

Valentine's Day was another story, one that has unfolded and transformed over the years since Rod died.

Rod usually took me out to dinner and sometimes sent me flowers and/or chocolates. Other than those things, it was like any other day – he went to work, I homeschooled the kids and did whatever else I had on tap for that day. But I was good with this because he also would take me out to dinner on Tuesday, or if I pouted.

But without my romantic partner, it seemed that I was somehow disqualified from Valentine's Day. Excluded for a reason beyond my control.

At first, it made me mad to see pics of everyone "celebrating each other" on social media. I remember avoiding social media altogether from the time I went to bed the night before til after I got up the day after. I wasn't mad at the folks for doing their thing; I just didn't need to see it. Seeing all those happy couples was like getting slapped in the face, pointing out what I no longer had.

Then I began to be irked at the expectations of the day. I knew they existed, but because I knew Rod would take me out to dinner at other times – without the social pressure – those expectations didn't bother me. I even told Rod at one point that it'd be okay if we went out to dinner on another night if he'd had a particularly stressful day, but he felt he *had* to do it on the 14th so he didn't look like a cad when people asked what he did for Valentine's Day.

And these expectations seem to lean more on the husband than the wife. I mean, I don't recall being asked where I took Rod for dinner or what I got him for Valentine's Day. There is plenty of photographic evidence of men fulfilling their socially dictated duty.

After anger and irritation, Valentine's Day became more of an annoyance. This may have been part of my growing awareness of social expectations in general and the often blind way people follow them – including me. But now that I am without a specific role or script to follow, these expectations land on me differently; it seems like it's more about money than love, more about impressing others than genuinely expressing your feelings to someone you care about.

No longer being part of the whole Valentine's Day thing, I was free from its expectations. The hype leading up to it – from chocolatiers to jewelers and florists, from vacation packages to greeting cards and cute heart-holding plushies – put unnecessary pressure on people to live up to some arbitrary standard set by "them," whoever "they" are. I mean, if someone is going to invest their time and resources into their relationship with me, I want to know that they are doing it of their own accord and that it's coming from a true heartfelt desire to do so rather than because it has been dictated or is expected.

Eventually I considered a different approach to Valentine's Day – it could be a day for expressing my affection and appreciation for anyone in my life. Romantic involvement is no longer a factor in this holiday for me, so I am no longer disqualified from joining in if I choose to do so.

I can also buy flowers or chocolates for myself on Valentine's Day if I want to. I know that I can do that any time, so if I choose to do it on February 14th, it's simply to take advantage of the abundant availability of these things.

At this point in my Valentine's Day story, I've gotten to the point that February 14th is just the day after the 13th and the day before my friend's birthday. I can make something of it if I so choose. Or not.

21

Birthdays

Birthdays were hard – his were harder than mine.

I missed getting presents from him and getting taken out to dinner on my birthday, but, as with Valentine's Day, my birthday was not the only time he did these things. Then, of course, that led to missing all the little things he did for me throughout the year. So the hardest thing about my birthday wasn't even about my birthday at that point; it was about missing *all* those things and times.

Rod preferred his birthday celebrations to be low-key. I tried unsuccessfully to throw him a surprise party on numerous birthdays over the years. I don't know if he was just that observant or if I was just talkative enough to give it away. Probably a combination of both, if I'm honest. But I did manage to surprise him at least twice ...

The first time was early on in our marriage; we were still in California. I got off work earlier than he did, and I spent that time before he got home decorating and getting ready to surprise him. I'd asked a number of our friends to arrive at our apartment before Rod got home from work. Everything was ready; the only ingredient left to add to this party was the birthday boy. He unsuspectingly opened the front door, got as far as his head and one foot in the door before hearing, "Happy birthday!" shouted at him. Upon seeing the small gathering in his living room, he stepped right back out and closed the door. We didn't quite know what to make of that, and there was a mix of stunned expressions and laughter. The door opened once again momentarily; we all broke out into laughter and he smiled as he actually came into the apartment. He was totally surprised – a feat I hadn't been able to pull off to that point.

The other time I got him was years later at a restaurant in Texas. I told him I was treating him to a special dinner at a hibachi table at a fancy Japanese restaurant. He knew I would have reserved two of the eight seats, but what he didn't know was that I'd reserved the whole table and invited some friends. When we got there, we followed the greeter as she escorted us to the table. As we approached, Rod recognized someone from around the corner and commented how odd it was that they'd be there the same night. It wasn't long before the table came into full view and he discovered the surprise. He stopped and looked at me with a look of utter disbelief for just a moment then his real smile took over his face. Even *I* can't believe I pulled that one off!

But those were the exceptions.

On just regular birthdays, I'd make a special breakfast – it just didn't seem right to send him off with his regular old oatmeal or cold cereal. It wasn't unusual for me to meet him for a cozy lunch for two, or to meet up with a group from work who were taking him out to lunch for his birthday. I'd usually have a special dinner planned, complete with a chocolate cake with chocolate frosting for his birthday. Thoughts of him would occupy my mind all day, and presents to wrap and food to cook would occupy my hands. Even though he was at work, he was still very much the center of my day.

After he died, I didn't know what to do with myself on his birthday. At first, I'd still cook one of his favorite meals for dinner, but it's just weird to eat and cry at the same time. Plus his favorite meals were often not my favorites.

On his fifth birthday after his death, I posted on his Facebook page asking his friends and family to share a special memory they had of and/or with Rod, and a lot of folks responded! It was really nice for me to actually see that he still existed in the minds and memories of other people. (I printed them all out and keep them in a safe place.)

But without him to focus on, it just seemed like any other day. Then that became the thing I was upset about. Not doing anything special on that day felt like one more thing about him, about his existence on earth, that was being erased.

I know cognitively that this is ridiculous. The responses I got on that Facebook post are proof that he's not being erased. But It still felt like the collection of tangible things that were evidence of his existence was dwindling.

I've come to accept that not celebrating his birthday since he passed is not erasing him, and that I don't need a body of evidence to prove to me that he's not erased from existence. What matters is that he is remembered.

22

Wedding Anniversaries

June seemed to be an eventful month for us, just in general. It was June when we got engaged, and a June two years later when we got married. It was June when Rod got a job that led to him working for EDS (Electronic Data Systems), where he'd work for the next 15 years. It was also June when EDS moved us to Texas. June seemed to be when we made large purchases (house, car) and, having spent whatever we might have otherwise spent on an anniversary trip or other celebratory event, we wished each other a happy anniversary and went on.

Our seventh wedding anniversary set us on a whole different track ...

I drove myself to the hospital early on the morning of our seventh anniversary to induce labor with Kristyn who was 18 days late and still showing no signs of being born any time soon. Rod brought the boys – who were five and three years old – to a sitter at a reasonable hour and joined me at the hospital later.

Labor progressed quickly. Rod had gone into the bathroom (in the labor room) to put on the medical garb he'd been given so he could be in the delivery room with me. They wheeled me out of the labor room while he was still in there. He was surprised to find an empty room when he came out; it took a minute for him to find where they'd taken me – and a minute was almost too long!

Just a few minutes after Rod found me, Kristyn was born! Because she was so long past her due date, she was immediately put into an oxygenated crib and wheeled away to the nursery. They said she'd need to be there for a few hours just to be sure she was breathing well. Once I was settled in my room, Rod headed out to grab a bite to eat and pick up the boys.

They finally brought her to me four hours later, and I got to hold her for the first time. When Rod came back, I handed him his daughter, wished him a happy anniversary, and said, "Top this!"

She became the unspoken part of every anniversary that followed. A private anniversary celebration – whether a nice dinner or a weekend getaway – would mean getting a babysitter. But I did not want Kristyn to be relegated to spending every birthday with a sitter.

Regardless of other birthday festivities, the birthday girl (or boy) got to choose what I made for dinner, and I made their favorite cake (or dessert), and we'd sing happy birthday on their actual birthday. (My boys' birthdays are 10 days apart; it was not uncommon for them to have a combined party. So having that special attention on their actual birth-days helped avoid making their individual birthdays into one single event.)

With this family tradition in place, it was difficult for us to celebrate our anniversary on our actual anniversary date. So, like our birthday dinner tradition, Rod and I started an anniversary tradition: having lunch together (instead of dinner) on our anniversary with a more formal celebration on another day.

Once Kristyn was in high school, we felt a little more free to celebrate our anniversary on the day of our anniversary. She (obviously) didn't need a sitter, but she also wouldn't be alone on her birthday ... at least not until her brothers moved out. After that it just felt wrong to leave her by herself on her birthday while Rod and I went out for a nice anniversary dinner. So one year, Rod decided that the three of us should go out together. Kristyn wouldn't be a third wheel; it would be a double celebration. He dubbed this new event our "birthaversary" and saw it as a way for him to celebrate both of his girls. We continued this tradition until he died.

That first birthaversary after Rod's death was weird for me, I must admit. **Should I still celebrate our wedding anniversary – even if he's not here to celebrate it with me? He may be gone, but I still married him all those years ago, and that was an important day in my life, one worth commemorating.** It was a day that began to shape me and gave my life meaning and purpose; his absence did not change any of that for me. But how do I celebrate a wedding anniversary solo? Should that date just go back to being just a birthday celebration, despite these things?

Kristyn and I decided to continue our birthaversary by going out to eat. Since that first one, we've added other activities that we both enjoy to do together. Sometimes we'd end up at Starbucks to include Rod in our celebrations – he loved coffee!

Besides taking me out to dinner, Rod always bought me an anniversary present. Knowing that he would be buying me a gift – and since I was already out buying birthday presents for Kristyn – I decided I would buy something special for myself, too. It felt a little weird, but I know he loved to spoil me, and that was enough.

At ten years out, my wedding anniversary is more personal, the focus of our birthaversary being more on Kristyn's birthday. I think sharing our anniversary with her all those years, and Rod combining them into a single celebratory event, has made it an easier transition for me.

I will always celebrate our anniversary, even if it is more internalized for me. Marrying Rod changed my life – it gave me purpose and direction, and fulfilled what I believed to be my destiny. It was a day that continues to shape my life even now, after fulfilling my marriage vows.

FIVE

Other Secondary Losses

"You can break and heal
at the same time.

They forgot to tell you that."

@MichelleBaumgard_1fw
(One Fit Widow)

23

Wedding Rings

I no longer wear my wedding ring, but it took about seven years for me to get here

Rod lost a lot of weight during his cancer treatments, so much so that his gold wedding band would literally just fall off his finger. So we got new matching bands, in silver this time. (Chemo is expensive!)

I had him buried in his new band, mostly because it fit him, and I continued to wear my matching silver band.

I watched my husband go from 160 pounds to 120 in just over seven months. I'm a small woman, and I thought to myself: *If I ever have to go through what he went through, I'd look emaciated in a very short time.* To solve this problem, I decided I was not going to worry about my weight. In fact, I was going to eat anything I wanted to eat and intentionally add some padding to my bones! I mean, I had no reason not to, there wasn't anyone I wanted to be attractive for anymore. Better to prepare for the unthinkable than worry about a dress size!

So I gained enough weight that my silver ring didn't fit comfortably anymore. It had been a couple of years at that point so figured I could just leave it off – no need to replace it.

Yeah, that lasted about a week. I didn't realize how much I played with it, how often it clanked against something and made a sound – sounds I didn't even realize it made until they were gone – and how naked I felt without it.

So I got myself a new ring. Not a new wedding band per se, but a band that was meaningful to me. So here's the story ...

Rod and I bought our gold wedding bands when we were 19 years old, a year before our wedding. It was our first purchase as a couple. "Our" song was "Always And Forever" by Heatwave, so we had *Always* engraved on the inside of my ring and *Forever* on the inside of his. We had to finance – for a year – the $300 for the rings and engravings!

A couple weeks before the wedding he decided to try his ring on; it was too small, and it got stuck. He tried all the ways to get it off to no avail. He finally had to tell me what was going on, and we went to the jeweler who had to cut it off! Luckily, we were able to get it resized in time for our big day.

The funny part of the story is that when they cut it off, they unknowingly cut it very close to the F in *Forever*, and in buffing out the addition of new metal, the F was also buffed away. So, from that day on, our rings promised *Always* ... *orever*.

The replacement ring I purchased has the words *Always*

and *Forever* on the outside, and a little infinity symbol between the words. I wore this ring until a few years ago.

I still have those gold bands, and I want to use both in a necklace. I have an idea of how I want them arranged, which is to have two holes made in his ring and the chain threaded through them so that his ring lays flat against my skin. My ring will be hanging free in a perpendicular direction on the small piece of chain that crosses through his.

I feel like this is a good representation of our marriage. I was enveloped by him while being able to move freely within that place of protection. Rod was definitely my place of safety and protection.

But for now they are still put away, waiting to be given this new life I have chosen for them.

About five years ago, I discovered spoon rings. I have collected a few from local holiday craft fairs mostly. I became obsessed with rings – spoon or otherwise – and wanted to get enough so that I could wear one on every finger if I so chose. I love it when they make sounds as I move my fingers and hands, even doing just normal things!

What I didn't realize as my collection of rings continued to grow was that wearing different rings on various fingers minimized the absence of a wedding band. After so many years of having that one single ring, not having it – or any rings – on was a dramatic change for me. And it just felt wrong, like I wasn't fully dressed. But if I had six or seven rings on both hands, I wouldn't feel so naked. And if my left ring finger was bare, it didn't seem to stand out as much, advertising that I was not married.

24

Future and Dreams

When I was little, I'd dream about my future – I'd find a good husband, start a family, and he'd provide for all of us, and we'd raise the kids to become well-rounded, educated, self-sufficient human beings. With Kristyn being the only kid still at home, that dream was nearly fulfilled.

Instead of going to college right after graduating from high school, she was gifted a horse, got a job to support said horse, and continued to live with Rod and I. She decided to go to college when she was 22, commuting her first year. The campus was about 60 miles one way, but she didn't mind the drive. She lived on campus her second year, but still drove home on the weekends and sometimes mid-week.

She found that she liked the little college town, so she devised a plan. During the second semester of her second year, she was going to scout out a little place to rent close to the campus, move there at the beginning of her junior year and finish out her degree. And who knew after that – maybe she'd blaze her own trail in that little college town.

At that point, the empty nest that always seemed so distant would soon become our reality.

Rod and I took this little bit of information, and we started dreaming of a different life.

We dreamed of living in a townhouse or condo type of community situation, one that had a workout room, business offices, walking trails, and a dog park. Of course, there would be a playground and pools for when the grandkids came to visit, and lots of space for them to run around outside.

We felt like that would be our time that we could just sit back and enjoy all that we'd accomplished. Rod was in a really good position at work, making enough for us to live comfortably. We were ready to shed the responsibilities of home ownership and property maintenance, and live somewhere where we can just enjoy the place.

We actually found the community we wanted to live in. Construction was just beginning when Kristyn started going to college, so it would be brand spanking new, high end everything, and the perfect location for us – right on her way between her college town and where her horses were boarded. It wasn't a bad drive to our offices ... which was a consideration since we would still be working a little longer before retiring.

I looked into the prices. At first, I got a little sticker shock, but when I compared it to all of the expenses of owning a home, it wasn't much more than we were paying for our current living situation. We were going to put in our application as soon as they were accepting them.

It was gonna be great. This yet-to-be-built place would have all the amenities, and we were looking forward to living there. And if that specific place didn't work out, we would definitely be looking for a similar type of situation in that general area.

Once he retired, Rod was going to focus on what had been a side hustle he started exploring about the time Kristyn went off to college. He called it "Rod's Voice." He was beginning to get involved in doing voiceovers and voice acting. His demo reel was aimed at radio commercials, announcer gigs and the like. You know that voice that says, "Welcome to the program. It is sponsored by ... Here's how you can support ..."? Yeah, he wanted to be that guy. He was also interested in doing audiobooks, too, and different things like that.

He bought a good microphone and other hardware necessary to record, as well as the proper software for recording and editing. He was already doing it on the side, mostly for free, as he was getting a feel for how everything would work. He went through an online training course, attended seminars and webinars, and he was part of an online voiceover community.

The idea was that once he retired from his regular job, he would build the voiceover business up a little bit, not to the point of another full-time job because, you know, he was retired! But it would be something he enjoyed, and he could do it for no other reason than that.

We talked about building him a little sound booth in the corner of one of our spare bedrooms using old accordion doors we'd taken off our laundry room and getting foam padding to soundproof it. We were going to make it portable so we could bring it with us once we were ready to move into our new "just us" place.

While Rod was honing his voice-acting skills, I was learning American Sign Language. I wanted to explore becoming a certified sign language interpreter so that in our retirement, I could take side jobs, too. As a certified interpreter, I could contact agencies for one-off assignments like a single event, or if somebody needed an interpreter for a wedding or a conference or something like that – those kinds of side gigs. I'd make a few dollars in the meantime. If I had an out-of-town assignment, Rod could come with me and we'd make a little vacation of it.

So I took sign language classes with plans towards getting certified. But, at that point, I was just starting to learn the language!

So those were the dreams we were getting ready to step into. We would be leisurely together and enjoy the fruit of our lives. We worked hard and accomplished a lot, and we were ready to sit back, sipping tea (or coffee) watching the sunset. If Rod had his druthers we'd sit and watch the sunrise – which I wouldn't be opposed to doing as long as I could go back to bed.

I also had my own idea of what growing old was going to be like for us. Whenever I'd see an old, white haired couple sitting on a park bench or holding hands while walking around the mall, or just being cute together, I just knew in my heart that that was going to be us.

Rod and I were going to be that cute little easy-going couple, just taking life one day at a time, taking things as they come. We were going to be that old couple in church who gets invited to the Young Marrieds Sunday School class to share our "wisdom" and how we'd put up with each other for over 50 years. And we'd be like: *I don't know, we just lived life.* And we were heading that direction.

That was the future I was looking forward to sharing with Rod. A future with side hustles and travel. We were going to go to Hawaii so I could see where he came from. We were going to go to Spain so he could see where my family came from. I don't know where else we might have traveled; for me the destination was really not the focus; it was the shared experience that I was looking forward to.

I imagined us taking care of each other when we were sick or after the inevitable and ongoing surgeries that seem to come with getting old. Making decisions for one another on health matters, or helping one another make hard decisions. We'd be there for each other for all of that.

And then, when we were old and had done everything we wanted to do, we would close our eyes together. We would be ready to say goodbye to one another, and we would be okay with that.

All those dreams died with him.

We were both 51, standing on the precipice of this new life.

That future that I had laid out in my mind, the one that I could imagine like photos in an album as though they had already happened, shattered. It's like they were beautiful scenes painted on stained glass windows that were shattered in a violent storm.

My future died with him. The future we dreamed together. The future I planned on ... that I believed would be my reality with every fiber of my being.

There was no Plan B. I think, maybe while he was sick, he tried to help me come up with one, but I wouldn't listen. Nope, I was praying for his healing, and the Bible told me that if I was going to get my prayers answered, I had to believe without doubting. Talking about him dying from this cancer felt like doubting to me. It was like saying to God, "Well I'm praying for him to be healed, but just in case..." No, that wasn't going to fly. I couldn't waver in my faith.

Since there was no Plan B, I did my best to continue with our Plan A.

We had been pretty much a one-income family, but his life insurance bought me some time before I'd have to go out and get a job to support myself.

If I was going to have to work full time, and since I was already planning on being a sign language interpreter, I decided to jump all in and go to school full-time and get that certification. That would be my second career – and my new source of income.

Making this decision to pursue my interpreter certification was me trying to follow through on our plan. He couldn't do voice-overs, but I could still interpret; it just wouldn't be the leisurely side job that I thought it would be.

Initially these classes were all about learning the language and learning the culture and the nuances of signing. It's not until you have a better grasp of the language that you can start to actually take the interpreting classes – voice to hands and hands to voice. It was in these classes that I came to realize this was not going to be a good career option for me. As an interpreter, I would be obligated to interpret exactly what was said, and the manner in which it was said. I realized that there might be some conversations (eg: violent, sexual, immoral, etc.) I would not want to be party to, or language that I would not want to repeat.

That's when that part of the dream died – nearly three years following Rod's death – because that's when I realized it was no longer something that I felt that I could do and enjoy. And I wasn't going to commit myself to doing something for the rest of my life that I wasn't going to enjoy. That's not how I wanted to live. Life's too short – I learned that lesson the hard way.

I still wanted to move into a condo or townhouse so that I didn't have the entire burden of house maintenance on myself, but I ended up moving into another house. That's when *that* part of our dream died.

I tried for a few years to continue moving forward in other aspects of *our* plan, but one by one, each step was completed, expired, or became irrelevant. My life was becoming so different without him, and the context that made our plan make sense didn't exist any more.

After ten years out, I still don't have a long-term plan, or even a dream for a specific future. I've gotten pretty good about being present and in the moment, though, because that's all I know that I have.

I do have a few plans – one of which is writing this book.

Since you're reading it, I've succeeded in that plan! But I don't know what comes next. Perhaps I'll focus on my blog ...

I'm just kind of here, focusing more on today than on a far off and uncertain future, more on being rather than doing.

Perhaps, that's where I need to be right now.

25

Grandparenting

Grandparenthood came early for us – Rod and I were both 48 – and we dove right in.

We got our parent upgrade in August 2010. I became Nonna, according to my Italian heritage, and Rod became Lolo for his Filipino lineage. The fact that lolo means "crazy" in Hawaiian (his other lineage) was a bonus – both of those designations fit him well.

For Christmas in 2012, we got a shadow box with a pink and a blue sock and other baby related items. It didn't take me long to figure out that we were going to have a second grandchild. Rod, on the other hand, took a little longer to decipher the significance of this particular gift. This little one was expected in May, 2013.

One month into Rod's chemo and radiation treatments, we went to the hospital to greet our new little granddaughter.

She was beautiful! Her eyes were not symmetrical, but it

was thought that it was due to her quick journey through the birth canal, and that it would correct itself pretty quickly.

When her eyes didn't even out as expected, doctor visits and tests determined that she had craniosynostosis, a condition that would require surgery on her skull to correct. The optimal time to perform this surgery would be before her first birthday.

Rod and I prayed for her and our family; we put her on any and all prayer lists we had access to. We talked about the upcoming surgery and he wondered if he'd be here when it happened. Believing with my whole heart that God was going to heal his cancer, I thought this notion absurd. Of course we'd both be there for her surgery, and for her recovery!

He died in Nov 2013; the surgery was still five months out. But it wasn't just her surgery and recovery that he was going to miss.

It was her starting to crawl, and her first steps.

It was her graduating from the bottle to sippy cups to eating with a spoon all by herself.

It was hearing her giggle, watching her wiggle-wiggle.

It was reading her stories in funny voices, and teaching her to block.

It was her first day of school, learning to drive, making a boy cry ...

It was her *whole life* that he was going to miss.

Having grandchildren was an experience that was meant to be shared between *two* grandparents. She was supposed to get the quiet cuddles from her Nonna and the goofily voiced stories from her Lolo; Nonna pushing her on the swings, and she chasing Lolo around the playground. We were supposed to tag team when she was over for an extended time. (We were young to be grandparents, but not *that* young when it came to chasing toddlers!)

Yet every time I held this sweet baby, it was like her whole growing-up raced through my mind – all the things Rod would be missing. I couldn't see her for her; all I could see was everything her Lolo would never see.

When it came time for her surgery, I was there, along with her other set of grandparents. I remember their presence together magnifying Rod's absence. My brain kept screaming,

*"There should be **four** grandparents here!"*

*"There should be **FOUR** grandparents here!"*

It just repeated over and over in my head; it was so loud. It was difficult for me to focus on the precious baby in my arms. As my tears flowed, spilling onto the little blanket she was wrapped in, I sensed that somehow she was absorbing all of my grief into her own little self. This was not something I wanted to put on her; it was not her burden to bear.

In the months before her surgery, I wouldn't turn down any opportunity to see her and her brother, and I did my best to put my grief aside during those visits. I did pretty well playing with her, going to the park, or regular daily activities (diapering, bathing). It was the quiet moments, like giving her a bottle, cuddling up to read a book, or snuggling down for naptime, that I just couldn't do without a heaviness about me; I couldn't separate my grief over Rod from the joy of having her in my life.

After her surgery, the mingling of my emotions and their transference into her became painfully evident, and the only way I knew to not transfer my grief onto her was to create emotional distance between us.

It broke my heart *to* hold her. I knew pouring my grief into her would not be doing her any favors, but all the moments and experiences she and her Lolo would never share ran rampant through my mind over and over, like a looped video that I couldn't stop.

It broke my heart *not to* hold her. I love her so much, and I knew I wanted to be an active part of her life, as both of my grandmothers were in mine. I also knew emotional separation would not be conducive to such a relationship.

I desperately wanted to be present with her, but my grief demanded my full attention.

There was a growing awareness in me that if things had continued as they were going, she'd lose both her grandparents, and I wasn't ok with that. This got my attention and prompted me to find a way to stop that looping video – or at least lower the volume so it didn't drown out the joy. It taught me to look for ways to hold *both* heartbreak *and* joy so that I could connect with my granddaughter and experience the joy of being her Nonna while holding space for my own grief.

My third grandbaby arrived five years after Rod died. I don't think any of them will know their Lolo beyond the stories I and their parents will tell of him.

I've always favored my Grama (my dad's mother). In terms

of stature, we are both barely over 5' tall and of a small build. My shoulders are square like hers were, and my hair is turning the same white as hers did. I learned a lot from her example about how a "lady" should think and behave, so I was a lot like her when it came to my beliefs about who I should be and about my place in the world. And while she seemed perfectly content – and capable – to be on her own, that was one way I never thought I'd be like her. Until Rod's diagnosis.

While he was still in the hospital, Rod held my hands in his, looked me in the eye, and with a smile that was meant to be comforting he said, "I guess you really are like your Grama."

Not only was I *not* comforted by this, but I felt the need to correct him ... "She was 59 when my Grandpa died, dude. You owe me eight more years!"

I've thought about this statement often since he died. At the time, I felt like he was trying to prepare me for his death, like he'd already accepted that reality and was trying to help me to come to that acceptance. But was there more to it than that?

My Grama never remarried. Was he hinting that he didn't want me to remarry after his death?

She lived almost 30 years on her own after my grandfather died, taking care of business, and being kind of bad-ass for an unmarried older woman in the 1960s and 70s. Was Rod telling me that he believed I would be strong enough to live like she did after he was gone? Was he telling me that he believed I was a bad-ass, too?

Or was he thinking about our grandkids, and telling me that he believed I would be able to have the kind of relationship with them that my grandmother-without-a-grandfather had with me?

Whether Rod meant it that way or not, I suppose I will be like her in that way, too. Having no memories of my own of my grandfather, I don't remember ever feeling like I missed having him. It was just me and Grama, and that was enough for me.

I'd spent two weeks with her every summer, just kinda living her life alongside her. We'd walk to the store with her little wheely cart, and play on the shuffleboard courts outside the laundromat while our clothes washed. We'd stay up late every night to watch the fireworks show at nearby Disneyland. We'd sleep in her room mostly, but sometimes she'd pull out the sofa bed in the living room, and I got to stay up late and watch Johnny Carson and eat Cheetos in bed. I loved spending time with her!

I wonder if she ever thought about what I was missing out on, what it would have been like if Grandpa was alive.

I know what my own grandkids are missing. Not only from my experience with my Popi, but from that very small window of time when I got to watch my husband and the father of my kids become Lolo.

I think at first I tried to be like Lolo in some ways alongside being Nonna, but I quickly realized that that wasn't my role, or my responsibility. (And that I was not very good at it.) I found that it just added to my own grief which then interfered with my ability to just be Nonna! So I leaned into my own role, finding my own connections with all three of my grandbabies.

I got to have Nonna-camps a couple of summers with my

two oldest grandbabies before they moved out of state. I'd get each one alone for a whole week. I took my little grand-daughter to get mermaid hair and make-up – complete with glitter. And I took my grandson to the Frontiers of Flight Museum. And they both got to pick their own new friend from Build-A-Bear Workshop®. We had other outings and did other things at home, too.

Since my youngest grandson lived locally, the whole family would come over now and again, and we'd all hang out to-gether. Until one day when my grandbaby asked his parents if they all could go to Nonna's house and then they (just his parents) leave. So his parents would drop him off one day every other week (we were still in a pandemic). And just like that, Nonna Days were born!

It is my hope that my grandkids will have memories of me that are complete in and of themselves, like the memories I have with my Grama.

26

Locus of Control

As I was dusting one morning, I found myself standing before a painting Ryan had painted for Rod that has a scripture on it: "My son, if your heart is wise, then my heart will be glad. Proverbs 23:15." As I read these words, I thought to myself: *I wonder if my son ever wonders if his dad would consider his heart wise now, and be glad.*

That query, in that context, was immediately met with another though: *Is Rod my son's standard? Is it appropriate that he should weigh his actions against whether or not Rod would be glad?*

Then it hit me – *is it appropriate that I should continue to weigh my own actions and decisions against whether or not Rod would be glad, or if he'd approve or disagree?*

It used to be that I'd check in with Rod when trying to make a decision or synthesize new information. His input informed my decision – he was my locus of control.

Without his input, I was lost. Hard as I tried – and believe me, I tried – I could not conjure up (or pretend to know) what Rod might have said in a given situation. I always felt like I was lacking pertinent information, like I was half a person. It was overwhelming and added to my feelings of inadequacy, my incompleteness as a human being.

And then the thing I was trying to do or decide was no longer the thing. That he wasn't here – his voice, his perspective, his support – became the thing.

As time went on, I questioned whether or not his input was still relevant in my current situation. Here are some examples:

We always kept our bedroom door closed because he didn't like our pets in our bedroom, especially at night. Since he died, I not only leave the door open all the time, but I also moved the dog's bed into my room, and the cat curls up with me on my bed at night. I find comfort in their presence; hearing the dog breathe (snore) and the cat purr (and snore) helps me feel not so alone at night.

But keeping the door open and having the pets sleep in my room felt really wrong at first, even though I found comfort in it.

Because Rod worked a regular 9-5 job, we all ate dinner together at about 6 pm after he got home from work. Eating dinner at that time was relevant to the life we were living, and it made sense in our context. I continued this schedule for some time after he died even though the necessity for it no longer existed. But having a sandwich or piece of fruit for dinner felt like I was being a disobedient child, rebelling against the rules. But that 6 pm dinner 'rule' was in place to accommodate a 9-5 work schedule that no longer exists for me.

When I visited Spain, I learned a different way of eating; they have their big meal around 2 pm and a smaller meal later in the evening. I liked eating this way, so I tried to continue this pattern when I got home. In this mode, a sandwich and piece of fruit at what would have been 'dinner' time was no longer breaking the rules; it was just following a different set of rules!

I didn't stick to this eating pattern very long either, but I learned something in the process: I learned to listen to my body, not the clock. As a result, I have a hard time designating which 'meal' I'm having at any given time because "breakfast", "lunch," and "dinner" each have their own timeframe for when they are eaten. Even what (and how much) foods are appropriate for each meal are wrapped up in these labels. What is it called if I eat at 9 pm, or if I have a full-on plate of food at 3 pm? I find that I am not only moving away from the mealtime rules I used to follow, but I'm also moving away from labeling them. I eat when I'm hungry and I eat until I'm full.

Every morning, Rod played "Mike and Mike," a sports radio talk show, on his iPad as we got ready for work. I liked having it on because it afforded me the vocabulary to participate in a different kind of conversation with Rod and it brought me into a different aspect of his world. After he died, I found their show on TV (who knew they actually televised their talk radio show!) and continued to listen to it every morning as I got ready for my day.

Since I no longer had anyone to talk with about it, and that had been its main appeal for me, it became background noise. But that was better than turning it off completely because not having that backdrop to my morning felt wrong, too; it didn't feel like my house without it.

When I quit my part time job to go to school full time, my morning routine changed. Not being a morning person, I selected classes that started later in the morning and even in the afternoon on some days; my 'mornings' didn't happen in the morning any more – well, at least not when 'morning' used to be.

Shortly after starting school I moved into a new (to me) house, so my environment changed. "Mike and Mike" never existed in this place. And since my reason for listening no longer existed, I never sought to bring them with me into my new place, into my new schedule.

After a time of quiet mornings with no musical backdrop, I have discovered that I like to listen to soft jazz after I get up and while I fix my first meal of the day (whatever time that may be).

He was my locus of control, the thing that determined my decisions and behaviors, for these and many other things that had context and relevance in our lives together. These were the rhythms and sounds of our family and our home; they were safe and familiar and comfortable.

But that external locus of control has been removed from me. This realization has not come in some great epiphany that allowed me to instantly operate from an internal locus of control. Oh, no no no.

It was a whole bunch of small moments spread out over time, many of which were met with resistance because each one felt like one more thing about Rod that was gone, one more way he was slipping away. They were moments like:

- Deciding that leaving my bedroom door open and having my pets in my room is an option.
- Realizing that it's ok if dinner isn't ready at 6pm, and I don't have to have rice with every meal.
- Realizing I don't have to watch movies in the theater, I can wait for them to come out on DVD, and I can still hear my TV just fine without the surround sound and graphic equalizer.

Some moments seemed bigger and more overwhelming ...

- I have to pay someone to fix my computer now rather than having my resident "IT Guy" fix it.
- It was completely up to me to decide when and if to trade in our car and make the decision to purchase a new one – and which one to purchase.
- A judge had to appoint me as executor so I could sign for Rod to sell our house.
- I have to check *what* box on this application form?!?

Other moments seemed to offer some freedoms ...

- I can quit my job and go back to school.
- I can travel to Spain to see an entire branch of my family I've never met before!
- I can paint my bedroom – my whole house for that matter – any color I want to!

This sounds like it'd be a good thing, doesn't it? To suddenly have the option to do whatever I want – without having to stop to consider someone else in these decisions.

I suppose it is, now. But it wasn't an easy road getting here; it came with a cost. Every one of these things was tied somehow to Rod, and choosing to change any of them meant I was letting one more evidence of his presence on this earth – and in my life – slip away.

So, to answer my earlier question, I'm pretty sure Rod would not approve of me letting the animals into my room, or that I may eat dinner at 4:30 – or 8:00 pm, depending on my mood or my tummy – or have a bowl of cereal for dinner. But I like to think that he is glad that I am weighing my own actions according to my own standards and not his.

I continue to live into the reality of having an internal locus of control, and developing that skill.

Which is actually a good thing.

27

Decision Making

Before I talk about how my decision-making processes were impacted by Rod's death, I want to address something I heard more than once, and said in great earnest, in my early days after loss: *Don't make any big decisions in the first year.*

Given the lostness and brain fog that came with being widowed, I latched on to any and all advice or guidance I was offered, accepting it all as valid and useful – including this little gem. I figured the ones who said this knew what they were talking about.

This advice gave me the impression that there was something magical about hitting that first year mark. That something was going to happen that day that would change my whole widow experience for the better; that life would suddenly be back to normal, like flipping some switch somewhere, if I could just hunker down and make it through that first year.

I did my best to follow this advice, but I wasn't able to; I sold my house and was all moved into my new home before hitting the ten month mark. There was a part of me that was holding my breath, waiting to see what the consequences of taking such drastic action in that first year would be. Guess what? There weren't any. At least none that waiting a couple of months would have made any different.

I now believe that this advice is actually acknowledging widow-brain, that fogginess that comes with being overwhelmed with grief and change and all the secondary losses that roll in like the tide. It's encouraging people to wait until that fog lifts and they are able to make decisions based on clear thinking rather than letting grief make decisions.

But it erroneously assumes a universal length of time for that fog to lift rather than understanding that grief becomes part of us – something we learn to feel and allow to heal. It changes us from the inside out and for the better, if we let it.

So, if you've been given that advice, apply it as is best for you. In my experience, there was nothing magical about reaching that first year mark.

Now on to my own decision-making process…

My life as a kid was pretty much decided by my parents – not unlike most kids, from my perspective. My parents decided where I went, when and how I got there, what I wore … When I got to be a teenager, I had a little more say in the matter, but I was still subject to the 'because I'm the parent' factor – I had to listen or there'd be consequences, right? So I was not solely responsible for making many of my own decisions as a kid or teen.

In addition to these 'lessons' in my childhood, I had a personal experience that shattered my trust in my ability to make decisions by and for myself.

It was the decision I made for myself at age 13 to follow Jesus. I was told that that decision was secure, that I did not need to doubt or question it. I believed this, and I felt secure in my decision.

As a teen, I went to church youth camps over several summers. But I had a very specific experience at one youth camp in particular when I was 16.

The campground was up in the mountains in Southern California. There was an area where they held all their services where we all gathered multiple times a day for worship music, the teaching of God's word, and whatever other events required everyone to be in one place. The designated place for these gatherings was built into the side of the mountain, creating a natural amphitheater amongst the trees. The sound was insulated so we could be as loud as we wanted with the music and the cheering and whatever else was going on.

A small group of us were hanging out during our free time one afternoon, and we stopped to get a soda at the cantina. It was oddly empty and quiet, and the guy who was working there was cleaning up. He looked up at us and said, "Oh, sorry, we're closed. It's time for you to get to the evening worship service."

We hadn't realized what time it was, so we shifted gears and headed for the amphitheater. I decided I needed to make a stop at our cabin before heading out. So while the rest of my little group headed down the mountain, I headed up to my cabin.

I passed a few people making their way to the service as I was heading to my cabin, but when I came out and started walking towards the amphitheater, there was no one around. Not a soul. I was calling out to anyone, but no answer came. I was listening for the sounds of the service, but I didn't hear a thing.

I don't remember if I got lost or if my cabin was just that far from the worship center, but it seemed to be taking longer than it should have to get there. I wandered long enough that I started to panic.

I was convinced that Jesus had come back in the rapture and taken up all the students and counselors and workers at the camp. Except for me.

I was terrified.

I eventually found the amphitheater with all my Christian brethren, and I eagerly joined them in the worship and Bible teaching time that was already under way.

It's quite possible that this event became evidence to me that my decisions could not be trusted. I had made the decision to trust Jesus as my Savior, but in that instant, I was uncertain that *that* decision was true, even though I believed it was genuine. Clearly, I could not be trusted to make my own decisions ... not even to save my own life.

Between this experience and the social norms I had observed up to that point, I learned two things. First, I needed to present my decisions to someone else for approval/validation; by themselves they were often flawed or not well-informed enough. I was not capable enough to consider all the factors, meaning my decisions were unable to stand on their own. Secondly, I could not trust decisions I made on my own, no matter how sure I felt about them.

When I went to college, I gained some freedoms in making decisions for myself, but they were made within a framework that was put in place by someone else. The decisions before me (which classes to take and when) were curated so that I would achieve a predetermined outcome (a degree).

I got a job after I quit college where I had decision-making authority, but I quickly realized that even that authority was limited. My decisions were still subject to my superiors' approval and/or correction, and could even be overridden by them.

When I got married, I believed my husband was the head of the household, and I was to be submissive to him. While I had the freedom to make decisions, they were now subject to my husband's authority, but in a different way than I'd experienced before. My decisions weren't so much subject to his approval or disapproval; it's more like they were incomplete without his input. That was all part and parcel of being married – I was part of a unit, and happy to be so.

If I wanted to get the most complete picture of a thing, I needed to see all sides of it, right? I can stand in front of an elephant and take a picture of its face and head, but that won't show me what the backend looks like. If I want to know what the whole elephant looks like, I have to look at it from the front, from the sides, and from the back. But I can only see what I see.

Rod was almost always standing in a different place than I was because he had a different set of life experiences: he was a man, he was a minority, and he grew up in an abusive household, to name a few. All of these things added up to create a very different perspective, and I valued that perspective. **I believed we knew more between us than I could know alone. We learned to rely on one another and our combined insights and experiences to make well-informed decisions for whatever it was we were deciding on.**

Because we each saw a different side of any given thing, putting our perspectives together gave us both a better picture, enabling us to make a more informed decision. I learned to trust this process (rather than my single-sided perspective) because I understood that my knowledge was limited, and I recognized my own potential for error.

This was how I learned a good decision was made: gather all the information that was available, talk it over with someone else to gain further insight, then come to a consensus to make a well-informed decision.

As a widow, I am no longer part of a unit. I am no longer part of my parental family or part of my own core family (because my kids are all grown). I am no longer a student, an employee, or a partner in a marriage. I am an individual. This is new to me because I never had to learn how to make decisions without getting outside input and/or seeking someone else's approval or validation. I'd never operated from an internal locus of control.

My biggest loss in the decision-making process was the conversation that either confirmed or altered my own thoughts or conclusions. That was a necessary element for me to confidently make a well-informed decision.

After Rod died, I felt like I was speaking to dead air. I would sit down with a decision to make; I'd say my piece but there was no response. No new information to consider, no other perspective, no affirmation of my own thought process. Just silence.

Imagine someone was right there when you started talking to them. You might have looked away or looked down momentarily while you're talking, but you just kept talking because they are still there. Then you look up and realize they've left, so you just stop talking mid-sentence, wondering where they went and how long they've been gone!

Or imagine you're at the bottom of the stairs, not realizing that there's one more step. You're expecting to land on level ground with your next footfall, but your foot just drops to the ground. It's jolting!

That's what it felt like every time I had to make a decision. **There was silence where there used to be another voice. There was an emptiness, an aloneness in the decision-making process without that voice.** I would think through all of my thoughts, but it was like speaking out into a void. There was nothing, not even an echo; just this empty space. Without that conversation, there was no other perspective presented, no alternatives to consider, no one with whom to come to a consensus. And without that, I was stuck.

I wasn't stuck in all my decisions. I made small decisions on the regular both before and after Rod died. I consider a decision as small when its consequences are limited and short-lived. For example, what I choose to wear today is of no consequence tomorrow. If I make a poor dietary choice, it can be easily corrected by the next meal, and any related unpleasant consequences (allergic reaction, upset tummy, etc.) usually work themselves out pretty quickly.

For me, a big decision is one that has consequences that reach beyond the decision itself. For example, selling the house involves more than a change of address. It will require further decisions like where to shop, what route to take to work and how long it will take to get there, or what schools the kids will attend. Other big decisions would be changing jobs or going back to school. All of these decisions carry a myriad of other decisions that come alongside and follow them. These were the types of decisions I needed help making.

So I began to seek other voices to fill that void – voices to provide me with insights and a perspective that I lacked. The subject of the decision would dictate who I might go to for that other voice, who I thought would be best equipped to help. Sometimes it was Rod's brother or my brother, sometimes it was one of my kids, or a good friend. But I still sought to fill that void by finding another voice that could bring to my attention things that I may have overlooked or missed, things that might affect my final decision. That worked. It helped get me unstuck.

For a time, asking others for input became my default rather than staying stuck. I was aware that whoever I would ask was not responsible for the decision, and they were probably, in a lot of these cases, not personally impacted by the decision. I mean, most people were not affected by whether or not I traded my car in and what car I got in its place, you know? But their perspective, their input, was helpful to me in making it.

I think that was a positive (and possibly necessary) step for me. It was a way for me to become unstuck; no decisions were being made in that void. There was only non-commitment and uncertainty. All those thoughts and ideas hung in the air, waiting for a response that never came. And with no response, there was no discussion. With no discussion, there was no decision.

Eventually I began to ask myself what I was still lacking that was causing me to continue to look outside of myself to make decisions. I began to ask questions of those who had been my stand-in voices: how did they make decisions, what was their criteria in making them, and how did they know which was the right decision or the best option.

I began to build my own decision-making muscles by trying out the different things I learned from them. One of these folks told me that you make a decision based on what you know. Sometimes it turns out to be the wrong decision, but that's okay, because oftentimes – most times – there's a way to correct it. You can either change the decision before the action's been taken, or even afterwards in some cases.

For example, if it involves a purchase and you decide after-wards it was not a good purchase, you can cancel the order. If it's too late to cancel it, you can return the thing. And if it's not returnable, you can sell it to recoup some of the cost or donate it.

Another example: Let's say you're planning a trip and you decide to rent a car because flying is too expensive. But then if you find some flights that are on sale you can cancel the rental car and book the flight.

Most of the time there's going to be a way to change a made decision, to make a different decision. It might be a little bit of a hassle and it can make things a little more com-plicated, and there could be some cost involved – whether it's money or time. But most decisions that you make can be unmade or altered.

And so it was very insightful to have someone else who I considered a very strong decision maker in his own right tell me that sometimes his decisions aren't the best ones, and that sometimes he has to go back and change a decision or make a different one altogether. It gave me confidence to make the best decisions I could based on the information I had, even if I still felt like I only had half of it.

I learned to give myself grace, and permission to say: *I can only know what I know.* And acknowledging that I can't make a decision based on things I don't know, I learned to extend compassion to myself when I had to change a decision. That step was really helpful in the whole process.

This process of learning to trust myself to make decisions is not a short one, and it is not easy. I still do not consider myself a strong decision maker in the same way that Rod was, but I have gotten to the point that I can actually make decisions rather than be paralyzed by them. I've learned to consider everything that I *can* see, everything that's within my scope of understanding and vision and realization, and then make the best decision I can with that information. And if I get new information, or it turns out not to be a good decision, I've gotten to where I'm okay with changing it and giving myself that grace. Maybe the fact that I made a decision at all is the best thing about that decision.

Learning how to make big decisions by and for myself is an ongoing process, and I've experienced a lot of growth through it all. Growth in self confidence to where I no longer need that external voice in order to make most decisions. I am no longer stuck in that void.

There are times that I do still seek an outside voice, times when I think it would be helpful to have another opinion, perspective or viewpoint. But when I find myself thinking that, I take that as an opportunity for self reflection. What is it about me or about this decision or this moment that makes me feel inadequate to make it? And what can I do to validate my own decision rather than look for someone else to validate it?

This is a place that I never sought to be (while I was married) because it was never a place I needed to be. Being of "one flesh," I believed that decisions were to be made together; with that being a part of my belief system, of course I wasn't going to make decisions by myself.

But without Rod, that belief system broke down; it no longer supported me. In fact, it became debilitating, paralyzing. In my journey to become a better decision-maker, I have had to let go of the belief that there had to be a consensus or mutual agreement with someone else for a decision to be made.

I gotta tell you, this belief was so ingrained that I wasn't even aware that it existed. I thought it was just reality – it's how things are. The sky is blue. I don't think of that as a belief; I think of that as a reality. And so it was just the same way with this – it was just a reality for me that my decisions were open for (or even required) discussion, and were subject to the authority of another person. Trying to undo that belief is like trying to undo the belief that the sky is blue.

But I have slowly made progress towards creating a new belief that external factors are not necessary in order for me to move forward with a decision. My new belief is that I have tools at my disposal to be able to make wise and informed decisions on my own – tools like Google, YouTube, and professionals (plumbers, electricians, etc.) that I can call. And of course my family and friends are still there for me, if I need them.

Every time I make a decision on my own, I take note of it and give myself a little pat on the back. Each of these victories – whether big or small – becomes part of a growing body of evidence that I can recall to help reinforce my new belief. They are evidence that I am learning not only how to make decisions on my own, but to trust myself to make them. I am learning what it's like to be an individual, and not be subordinate to anyone. I am learning that I am enough.

This process has helped me grow as an individual. And growth in this area is huge for me because I've never had a time in my life where I operated as an individual, where I was self-sufficient. And as that body of evidence continues to grow, so does my confidence in making decisions.

28

Conversations

Conversations are a secondary loss for me. I'm not talking about the loss of conversations Rod and I had on a daily basis, though those are a secondary loss in and of themselves.

I am talking about conversations that I will never get to have with him.

Rod was an intellectual. He had a wide variety of interests, including but not limited to philosophy, theology, and mythology. He was well-versed in these subjects, and he liked to talk about them. And I loved to listen to him talk about them. I didn't spend a lot of time reading about any of these things, except perhaps theology, and that came in the context of church – Bible studies, sermons, Sunday school lessons, things like that.

When the boys were in high school, we used a home-school curriculum called World Views of the Western World

(Cornerstone Curriculum) which was heavy in philosophy and theology. Required reading included a lot of the great philosophers' works that didn't necessarily reflect a Christian worldview; the whole point of the curriculum was to take in what you hear and use critical thinking skills to weigh it against the plumb line of the Bible. So, they were exposed to a lot of classical and modern philosophical and theological ideologies.

I would listen to Rod engage with the kids about what they were reading. I loved listening to their conversations, but I never felt like I had anything to offer. I had not taken the time to study the topics and to form an opinion of my own to add to the conversation. I was completely the learner in that scenario, and even then my interest stemmed from a desire to spend time with Rod rather than the acquisition of knowledge.

There was no practical application for me in that knowledge. I wasn't going to go teach a class or participate in another discussion where I'd be able to share that information with anyone. I wasn't even on a journey of personal exploration; I felt like I got all of the theology I needed from church, and any questions I had beyond that, Rod was able to answer. And I was happy with the arrangement. I thought their conversations interesting, but they weren't really conversations that stayed with me much beyond the moment. I was invested in the participants, not the content.

There were times when Rod would start a conversation with me about something in which his thoughts or musings were outside of my range of knowledge or my belief system. I remember snapping back, "Well, what about this bible verse?

And what about what our pastor said about it – how do you reconcile that?" I responded this way because I wasn't open to considering what he had to say. He wasn't going to argue the point; he wasn't trying to convince me of something or prove anything to me, he just wanted to have a conversation with me. My response clearly indicated that I was not open to having this type of conversation. Sometimes he would bring it back to the Scriptures to put it into a context I could accept for my benefit, but most times, he would just let it go. So the conversation he initially started – the one he wanted to have with me – was never had.

My belief system was my whole world. I didn't know how to consider the existence of anything outside of it because I believed that what was true for my world was true for the whole world. It was the whole truth, and there was nothing beyond it. Any time I was presented with something beyond it, I was not able to entertain it. Entering conversations like this with Rod was not an option for me. He had to bring the conversation back into my world in order to have this kind of conversation with me. And he so graciously did this with great patience (and regularity that I was not aware of, I'm sure).

Here's an illustration:

Whenever I watched someone use sign language, all I could see was the beauty in the movement. And I was astounded that this person over here was moving their hands and that person over there was watching and understanding. They were having a conversation, and it was all through their hands. But I understood none of it.

In those early experiences, the meaning of what they were

doing was lost on me, completely out of my hearing context. Nothing in my life, in my reality, could comprehend it. It existed outside of my world, outside of my context as a hearing person.

I could accept that it was a thing, but it was a thing for them. Because I accepted that there was another context in which to live, I was open to learning the language. I did not possess the skill or the knowledge to have a conversation in sign language when I started, but with each class I took, I gained understanding, skill, and perspective. I met deaf people, and I listened to their stories and learned what life was like for them as a deaf person living in a hearing world.

And I finally got to the point – with time, persistence and practice – where I could have a conversation with a deaf person. It was in accepting that a different context existed that I was able to gain an understanding of it, and then hold space for both of those worlds to exist at the same time.

When Rod was trying to have those deep conversations with me, it's like I was pre-ASL1. I was aware of the conversation, understood that it had meaning, but the meaning of it was lost to me. I was not ready to accept its validity, that it existed in the world; it was outside of my context.

Just like learning sign language took me out of my context as a hearing person, learning anything different about God or reality as I experienced and understood it would require me to take a step out of my context as a Western evangelical believer. And I wasn't able to do that. So when Rod tried to talk to me about things that existed outside of my context, I couldn't comprehend them.

It was about three years after Rod died that my world,

my perspective, my understanding of reality began to expand outside of what I had previously considered to be the whole truth, my whole world.

I took a great interest in spiritual things – the supernatural, if you will. (I mean, if you think about it, religion itself is supernatural because it deals with something that is beyond our world, beyond our plane of existence.) I took an interest in things beyond what the Western evangelical church teaches, and started questioning my own personal theology, exploring other philosophies, and listening to others' stories.

I started asking questions about who God is because the God that I believed in was not the God I experienced during Rod's illness, his death, and the aftermath. I got to a point where I was able to separate God from what I had learned *about* Him. I wasn't separating myself from God, but instead asking Him to reveal himself to me outside of the context in which I'd come to know a *version* of Him. I chose to be open when I encountered something different rather than dismiss it as woo-woo or even heretical. I chose – and am still choosing – to listen to my experience and the experiences of others, to my intuition, and to that still small voice that's inside of me as I continue to know the Divine.

I changed how I read the Bible. Instead of reading a passage with the thought that I know what it means and how it applies to my life, I chose to read the Scripture as though I was reading it for the first time. And it began to take on a different meaning for me.

I believe the reason it was able to take on a different meaning was because the Holy Spirit (or my intuition or higher self?) was teaching me something different than I had learned before *because I was finally open to learning it.* I had believed that Scriptures meant one thing for all people for all time, but I was beginning to experience its dynamic nature as the living Word of God! I might get a completely different understanding of a passage because I am in an entirely different place in my life than I was when I've read it before. And it might mean something different to someone who is in a different place in life, or has a different understanding of God. I now believe God can speak to anyone through anything and tell them anything they need to know. It has everything to do with how the person is receiving the Word, and how ready or open they are to receiving it.

So anyway, I have been questioning a lot of my religious beliefs, and God has been revealing Himself to me. And because I have put myself in a mode of acceptance, I have been able to see – and comprehend – what I'm being shown. My world has broadened, my context has expanded. My beliefs about God and the universe and how the world works have shifted.

I've also found other people's perspectives interesting – their perspectives on the Bible, on God, on Christ, on heaven and hell, on whatever – rather than silently judging those beliefs, or judging them for holding those beliefs. (By judge I mean thinking that they are lost and going to hell.) And I have opened up my heart to receive what God might reveal to me through any and all of these stories and venues.

As a result of being curious and open, I have read and studied a variety of philosophical and theological books and texts, and now I have very different thoughts about these things than I had before.

Now I'd have something to add to all those conversations Rod had with our kids all those years ago. And I'd be open to having the conversations Rod tried to have with me.

It's those conversations that I have lost – ones I could have been a part of with Rod, ones I missed out on when I had the chance, that I will never get to have with him.

Afterword

Secondary losses are hard; no one ever told me that the primary loss (losing my husband) was just the beginning of a whole string of losses. At first, the awareness of multiple secondary losses comes flooding in, emotions hitting like waves on a beach during a storm. And you feel helpless to protect yourself from them in any meaningful way when they hit from out of nowhere. You just sit there on the beach, getting pounded by the onslaught of water, sinking ever deeper into the sand beneath you, any hope of escape diminishing as the waves and sand envelope and incapacitate you.

Eventually the storm passes, giving you a reprieve, a moment to dig yourself out of the hole, brush off the sand, and try to figure out what just happened. Before you know it, the winds pick up and it starts all over, wind and rain beating you down into the sand again. But this time you know it will pass, so you hunker down, hold your breath and wait it out.

Next time, you find your feet a little quicker, and you begin to assess the situation. You realize that you can see the storm clouds off in the distance, so you begin to make a plan to prepare for the next wave of emotion before it hits. At first it's small, a single decision – find an umbrella. Then, with your umbrella and a bit of clarity, you may be able to see your way to one more small decision, and then another, each one a pebble of confidence as you find your way through the storms.

By the end of writing this book, I will have been a widow for ten years. In that time, I have learned some things about secondary losses. For one, I learned to see some of these storms approaching (like his angel-versary, holidays, etc.). Knowing these dates were approaching, I was able to make some decisions. At first they were avoidance decisions like taking a social media hiatus for Valentine's Day or going to church at my kids' church for Mother's Day – essentially removing myself from the oncoming storm. As the years have marched on, I've been able to make different decisions about these events, ones that have gradually moved beyond avoidance to bringing healing.

Another thing has to do with the less predictable storms. I am learning to live with my emotions, to actually feel them rather than deny or "stuff" them down. I am learning how to be gracious with myself, moving away from the idea that there are good emotions and bad ones (though there are ones that are more pleasant to experience than others), to accepting that all of my emotions are different expressions of me.

I guess you could say that I am learning to dance in the rain.

Do I have everything figured out? No, I don't. I don't experience secondary losses like I did closer to the original loss, but a song on the radio or driving past our favorite restaurant can still hit me with a wave of tears. I have learned to breathe through them and ride the wave.

Life is dynamic, and there will always be things to learn and ways to grow and heal. They like to say that time heals all wounds, but I don't believe this is entirely true. Time gives us space and opportunities for our wounds to heal; it's up to us to choose what we will do with those opportunities. But I believe it's in that place of healing that we begin to experience peace and to thrive once again.

Your journey will not look like mine, but there are things that we, as widows, likely have in common. I hope the conversations in this book have made sense to you; more importantly, that they have helped you make sense of your own journey.

It is my hope for you, dear reader, that reading about my experiences has given you hope. You are not lost; you are just on a path you've never been on before. But it's not an untraveled one. And once you're able to turn from looking behind at what's been lost to looking at where you are, you'll *see* that you're not alone out here. May you be brave enough to look forward, to see what lies ahead.

Wherever you are on your journey, be gracious with yourself. Allow yourself time to heal and space to breathe. You got this.

About the Author

Gail is a New York born California raised Texan. She married her high school sweetheart, had some kids, and shared all the things. After 30 years of marriage, and with an empty nest in sight, Rod was diagnosed with pancreatic cancer. Seven months later, on November 22, 2013, he passed away.

She has a blog (onecraftywidow.com) where she talks about being a widow as well as the deconstruction and reconstruction of her personal faith, and general observations about life after losing a partner. She received her Widow Coach certification in January, 2020. With time and healing, Gail has rediscovered fiber arts and paper crafts, has taken to doodling, and discovered she likes country line dancing!

Resources

ONLINE RESOURCES:

One Crafty Widow

This is my blog where I talk about my widow experience, my faith deconstruction and reconstruction, and general musings and epiphanies on life without a partner, and on life in general. www.onecraftywidow.com

Modern Widows Club

"Modern Widows Club is here to help widows transform their grief after loss into a positive, purposeful future while embracing their own strength and courage. Thereby building new friendships and community as they walk this path with their "Wisters" (widow+sister)." – ModernWidowsClub.org

VIRTUAL COURSES:

The Art of Grief

I was introduced to Linda Shanti McCabe, PsyD, R.E.A.T. (Registered Expressive Arts Therapist), through the Modern Widows Club Art Club, where she hosts monthly art sessions (free for

MWC members). We create a new SoulCollage® card each month to build our own deck. (Seena Frost, M.Div., M.A., SoulCollage® founder). I later participated in her online course, "Expressing the art of grief: a program for women whose person has died," an 8-week course exploring different modes and mediums of artistic expression to allow grief to process, to be released from our bodies.

You can find Linda at drlindashanti.com or ItsNotAboutThe-Art.com

JoAnn the Life Coach

Through the Widow Coaching Center membership and Widow Coaching Certification course, I gained tools to assess my situation and my state of being, and to shift my thinking to create a life that I want to live.

Find out more here: https://joannthelifecoach.com/about/

PODCASTS:

Healthy Widow Healthy Woman – Carolyn Moor (Founder of Modern Widows Club)

WidowCast: Widows Empowering Widows – How to Self Coach Through Grief – JoAnn Filomena (JoAnn the Life Coach)

The Widowed Mom Podcast – Krista St-Germain

The Widow Squad Podcast – Widow Squad

BOOKS:

On Grief:

A Grief Observed by C.S.Lewis, HarperSanFrancisco 2001 (Did you know he was widowed?)

On Widowhood:

Widowed: Moving Through the Pain of Widowhood to Find Meaning and Purpose in Your Life Again by Jo Ann Filomena, Moran James Publishing, 2017

On Faith/the Bible:

Out of Sorts: Making Peace with an Evolving Faith by Sarah Bessey, Howard Books, 2015

Inspired: Slaying Giants, Walking on Water, and Loving the Bible Again by Rachel Held Evans, Nelson Books, 2018

What Is the Bible: How an Ancient Library of Poems, Letters, and Stories Can Transform the Way You Think and Feel About Everything by Rob Bell, HarperCollins Publishers, 2017

On Living/Building a Life:

How to Be Alone A Poem by Tanya Davis, HarperCollins Publishers, 2013

Life's Golden Ticket: A Story About Second Chances by Brendon Bruchard, HarperOne, 2008

The Power of Now: A Guide to Spiritual Enlightenment by Eckhart Tolle, New World Library and Namaste Publishing, 1999